T0178716

SEO Management

SEO Management

*Methods and Techniques
to Achieve Success*

Véronique Duong

WILEY

First published 2019 in Great Britain and the United States by ISTE Ltd and John Wiley & Sons, Inc.

ISTE Ltd
27-37 St George's Road
London SW19 4EU
UK

www.iste.co.uk

John Wiley & Sons, Inc.
111 River Street
Hoboken, NJ 07030
USA

www.wiley.com

Library of Congress Control Number: 2019946163

British Library Cataloguing-in-Publication Data
A CIP record for this book is available from the British Library
ISBN 978-1-78630-459-9

Contents

Acknowledgments

Search engine optimization (SEO) has been my passion since 2010. I am a computer linguist engineer by trade and I became an SEO expert thanks to self-study. Today, I have made it a real profession and co-founded an international search agency in Paris. I regularly speak at events related to SEO, search and web marketing.

I decided to write a second book on SEO project management and SEO techniques covering several search engines (Google, Baidu, Yandex, Naver, etc.) in order to share and highlight a generic and broad approach to my methodology and support the large contingent of people interested in the field. I share my know-how and most of the main actions that make it possible to succeed in the rankings, the organic traffic and visibility of a site.

When I wrote my first book on SEO Baidu, I was also president of the largest SEO association in France, the "SEO Camp". With hindsight and in response to the current issues facing the SEO business, I would like to make the latter expand simply and correctly throughout the world.

That is also why I specialize in SEO on an international scale, knowing that speaking six languages helps me a lot.

I wish to dedicate this book to my parents and sister for their daily support, my associates Steve and Benjamin from Rankwell, my friends and social circle, current and former collaborators and my SEO mates.

Introduction

SEO: An Essential Traffic Channel

Search Engine Optimization is a well-known and recognized field (or sector or online marketing activity) for companies and organizations that want to succeed in their online visibility strategy. It is a complete field, where we find:

– technology, research and development, since search engines are constantly evolving and it is necessary to adapt to their technologies and systems;

– semantics, since the bases of SEO are the keywords and queries that Internet users have thought of and searched for in search engines;

– communication, since it is necessary to know how to write original, unique and interesting texts and content;

– marketing, since it is necessary to find external links with partners, and to know how to create relations, maintain them and have a good rapport.

The most well-known search engines are currently Google (which has a monopoly in terms of market share in most countries) and Baidu (mainly in China). The biggest brands rely heavily on these two engines to acquire traffic or visits and carry out transactions.

In this book, we will explain the technical, semantic and link building strategies to optimize a site, from A to Z. From the tag to the conversion, we will go into detail to help companies that want to be visible online achieve their objectives. In this book, we will share concrete examples in all the chapters on technical SEO and semantic SEO because we want to share recommendations that are directly applicable in the field.

A chapter will also be devoted to SEO project management in order to allow any expert or researcher in the field of SEO to carry out the necessary optimizations on a website.

Techniques related to automatic language processing will also be explained, such as TF-IDF (a statistical measurement used to calculate a score that determines which web page would be most likely to be positioned on a particular keyword), n-grams (which are sequences of words or characters used to detect duplicate content) and named entities (which represent linguistic expressions to determine the names of places, people, organizations, etc.). The latter are also used for voice search, a popular topic for the future of search engines, which aim to become response engines.

State of the Art of SEO

1.1. The market share of search engines

Before we talk about search engine optimization (SEO), we must first focus on the market share of search engines around the world. Indeed, in the West and Asia, we are not looking for information on the same engine. In European and English-speaking countries, the most widely used engine is the American Google. In China, on the other hand, Baidu is the most widely used. At the moment, Google and Baidu are the search engines with the highest market share in the world[1].

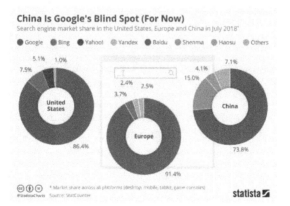

Figure 1.1. *Google and Baidu worldwide market share. For a color version of this figure, see www.iste.co.uk/duong/SEO1.zip*

---

1 "Google et Baidu, les deux géants de la recherche sur Internet", available at: https://www.journaldunet.com/media/publishers/1417975-google-et-baidu-les-deux-geants-de-la-recherche-sur-internet-selon-statista/.

Therefore, for these territories in the world, we must focus on Google and Baidu (and also its national competitors, such as Shenma, Qihoo 360 and Sogou). There are still other search engines for different countries in the world; here is the list:

– in Russia, there is Yandex, which has a fairly large market share with more than 50%[2], while Google has less than 45%;

– in South Korea, there is Naver, which has a market share of 25–30%[3] (Google possesses the majority);

– in Japan, there is Yahoo! Japan, a local search engine based on Bing's results in Japanese and which has an average[4] market share of about 30%, depending on the year (Google also has the remaining share of the majority in this case).

Every year, search engines evolve at faster and faster speeds. In this book, we will discuss SEO methodologies that apply to all search engines, since the different engines all have a common base: one or more bots (called crawlers or engine robots) that scan web pages, index them and then push them into search results in relation to a particular query.

1.2. Developed technologies and voice search

1.2.1. *Google AMP and Baidu MIP*

Since 2015, the two largest search engines in the world, Google and Baidu, have developed many technologies, such as AMP (accelerated mobile pages) at Google and MIP (mobile instant pages) at Baidu.

AMP and MIP aim to make the pages of mobile sites as fast as possible, so that they load in 3 sec maximum on smartphones and tablets.

---

2 "Yandex, les parts de marché russe en hausse!", available at: https://www. search-foresight. com/yandex-parts-marche-russe-hausse/.

3 "The most popular South Korean search engines", available at: http://blog.webcertain.com/ the-most-popular-south-korean-search-engines/01/03/2018/.

4 "Most Popular Search Engines in Japan: Google Japan vs Yahoo! Japan", available at: http://www.theegg.com/seo/japan/most-popular-search-engines-in-japan/.

Figure 1.2. *AMP in the West, MIP in China*

Google and Baidu wish to accelerate the Web, in order to take into account more and more data, to index them faster, with the objective that web pages represent the least possible use of their resources. To do this, the AMP and MIP versions of the sites are very refined: there is little JavaScript, few images and few CSS (cascading style sheets).

Figure 1.3 shows an example of a site in classic version and in AMP version[5] (Google).

Figure 1.3. *Classic web page versus AMP (or MIP) web page*

5 "Google et sa nouvelle règle AMP contre les utilisations abusives!", available at: https://www.araoo.fr/google-nouvelle-regle-amp/.

The idea of these new HTML AMP and HTML MIP languages is to include only the essential information on smartphone users' browsers. Advertisements, images and elements that are not important information for users are hidden or are not recalled in the mobile version in AMP or MIP.

Google focuses on AMP and is planning on deploying the technology in a major way from 2020. Baidu, for its part, announced that sites in AMP (the language developed by its American counterpart) could also be supported in their system[6]. The Chinese engine could then take into account both HTML versions, AMP and MIP.

1.2.2. *Voice search and connected speakers*

Voice search will become one of the most widely used channels in the West by 2020. We estimate that 70% of searches will be done using voice in a few years. According to a study conducted by SEMrush (a statistical tool for monitoring analytics), future searches will undergo a major change compared to current methods.

Figure 1.4 illustrates the primary representation of future search methods.

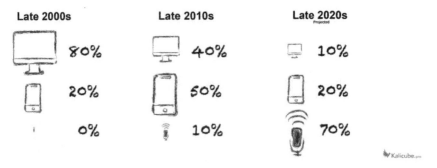

Figure 1.4. *Evolution of search methods and device use (image source: Kalicube)*

From 2020, the majority of us will be carrying out voice searches using speakers, such as Google Home, and we will use computers much less than before.

---

6 "Baidu becomes Google's biggest ally in mobile page speed", available at: https://search engineland.com/baidu-becomes-googles-biggest-ally-in-mobile-page-speed-271275.

Figure 1.5. *Google Home*

According to statistics and studies, there were more than 1 billion voice searches carried out in January 2018[7]. That is why our way of making recommendations or giving SEO recommendations must also adapt and change. We need to focus on featured snippets, knowledge graphs, local referencing with Google My Business, rich cards, rich snippets,[8] etc.

Schema.org has launched a tagging system for content for voice searches, with a structured data tag called *Speakable*. Its syntax is as follows:

```
< !DOCTYPE html>
<html>
<head rel="home" href="/" itemid=""  itemscope
 itemtype=http://schema.org/SpeakableSpecification">
<title>Example showing complex structures in HTML head</title>
<meta itemprop="cssSelector" content=".title" />
<meta itemprop="xpath" content="/html/body/h3" />
</head>
<body>
<h1 class="title">Complex Microdata in HTML head</h1>
<p>...</p>
</body>
</html>
```

---

7 "15 chiffres sur la recherche vocale qui interpellent", available at: https://www.arobasenet. com/2018/08/15-chiffres-recherche-vocale-4868.html.

8 Rich snippets: these are search results enriched with stars (reviews), product prices, event dates, or any element that can complement a search result in search engines.

Here are some recommendations proposed by Google for the Speakable tag:

– it is not necessary to insert the tag in complete content, but rather on certain precise and specific points that explain the general idea well;

– do not insert this tag on content that could create confusion when it is vocalized: photo caption, content source, geolocation, etc.;

– the content can be of two to three sentences (or 20–30 sec of audio content, once vocalized).

At the time of writing, Speakable is only available for U.S. English in the United States, but Google mentions that other language-country pairs should follow soon, depending on the success of this new possibility.

This tag is also only valid for sites included in Google News at the moment. Therefore, for a French site in the classic search part, the use of Speakable is not possible at the moment, but it is necessary to monitor its evolution in the years to come.

Figure 1.6 illustrates the trend of Google Home searches worldwide over the past 5 years (knowing that Google Home has been on the market since March 2016).

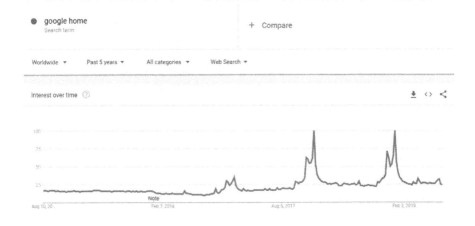

Figure 1.6. *Evolving interest in Google Home*

We notice that there is an interest in Google Home and that there are search peaks during the end of year holidays (because Internet users certainly use it to look for gifts).

In China and Asia, Internet users are already much less likely to be on computers and more likely to be connected to mobiles. With voice speakers like Baidu's Xiaoyu (小鱼在家) and Alibaba's Tmall Genie X1, voice search figures are likely to increase rapidly as well.

Figure 1.7. *Speaker with Baidu Xiaoyu Zaijia display*

Figure 1.8 shows the search trend for Baidu Xiaoyu, the voice speaker of China's leading search engine.

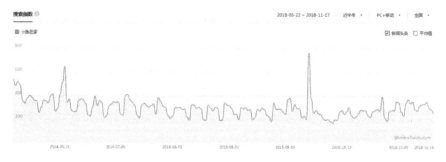

Figure 1.8. *Evolution of interest in Baidu Xiaoyu*

In China, we clearly see that Internet users have a real interest in voice search: we are talking about 400 searches per day on the Baidu Xiaoyu speaker. When we compare it with Google Home, on a range covering all countries and over the last 5 years, the latter does not demonstrate such large results.

If a company wants to do SEO in China using Baidu, it is necessary to think about voice search now.

On Google, we have search results at the very top of the results page (also called SERP [Search Engine Results Page]), which are called "featured snippets". These results are also considered to be classified as "zero position" or "0 position". These are what are spoken by Google Home.

Figure 1.9 shows an example of a featured snippet on the definition of the term language engineering.

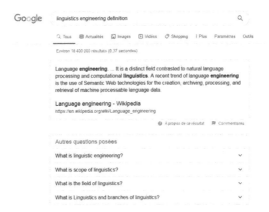

Figure 1.9. *Example of a framed zero/featured snippet position at the beginning of the result page*

It is now necessary to optimize web pages with techniques that allow sites to move up to position 0, so that Internet users can hear the answers to their questions asked orally.

In Chapters 3 and 4, we will come back to this case and explain how human–machine communication works at the moment, and how we can move to position 0 or featured snippet.

Since 2015, Google and Baidu have been carrying out regular research and projects. We have detailed the major projects for the coming years, projects that will have a concrete impact on society. Voice search will reach a large number of people in today's society and we must prepare for it now. Mobile-friendly web pages will also have a direct impact on everyone's daily life.

If we have sites that load faster on mobile phones, we can access information faster and also save time in the long term.

Google is still preparing projects on Progressive Web Apps and Instant Apps and launching new algorithms, such as Rankbrain (a semantic web and artificial intelligence algorithm that aims to provide more relevant search results for users, through semantic analysis and a network of more advanced semantic relationships). For its part, Baidu is working on several subjects: artificial intelligence applied to autonomous vehicles, voice speakers, MIP pages, etc.

The objective of this book is to outline the basic information on all search engines, and especially to teach a methodology for the management of SEO projects.

Our first goal is to explain concretely how to manage an SEO project and how to make sure that the web pages of a site are relevant for search engines, so that they generate organic traffic, and eventually conversions or transactions.

In Chapter 2, we will explain step by step how to manage an SEO project, then we will discuss technical SEO and semantic SEO in the following two chapters respectively.

## 2

SEO Project Management from A to Z

For each SEO project, as soon as we receive a specification or a brief from the client, we start the procedure to set up a SEO campaign.

In this chapter, we will take you step by step, in a concrete way, through the process of setting up an SEO campaign.

SEO is a set of technical, semantic and partnership actions aimed at improving the visibility of a website in search engines.

To set up an SEO campaign, you need to plan:

– technical optimizations;

– semantic optimizations;

– optimizations of external links (off-site SEO);

– plans for redirection, website cleaning, etc.;

– the writing of fresh and quality content;

– meetings and calls to ensure the smooth running of the project.

Figure 2.1 illustrates how SEO support can be articulated based on our experience.

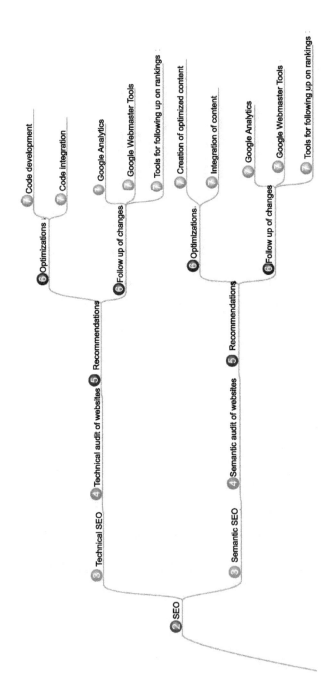

Figure 2.1. *Mapping of the implementation steps during an SEO project*

For any SEO project, we have specifications that list these major steps and what we must achieve within them:

– SEO audits (technical and semantic);

– optimizations;

– integrations;

– follow-up;

– strategic monitoring;

– monitoring of e-reputation.

2.1. The specifications or customer brief to be respected

SPECIFICATIONS

Administrative clauses

1. Market object
2. Legal and regulatory provisions
3. Execution method
4. Buyer power
5. Method of determining prices
6. Qualitative selection
7. Submitted content
8. Content of the offer
9. Storage of offers
10. Delay in validating an offer
11. Delay in market execution
12. Payment methods
13. Price revision
14. Other price elements
15. Anticipated termination
16. Lingua franca and meetings
17. Warnings
18. Subcontracting
19. Confidentiality
20. Property of results
21. Security
22. Reception
23. Penalties
24. Judicial actions

Technical clauses

1. Description
2. Execution modalities
3. CMS
4. Place of supply
5. Delivery

Appendices

Declaration on honor - Turnover
Bank declaration model
Inventory of services
Submission form

Design brief

COMMUNICATION...
1. INTERNAL INVESTIGATION CONCERNING THE WEBSITE PROJECT..
2. TARGET AND NEEDS ....
3. KEYWORDS ....
4. INFORMATION NEEDS...........................
5. MARKET..
6. SITE OBJECTIVES ....
7. LANGUAGE..
PREREQUISITES AND ORGANIZATION................
1. BUDGET...
2. DEADLINES..
3. PROJECT ORGANIZATION ....
4. ORGANIZATION AND ROLE......................
5. STATISTICS..
6. PLANNING..
DESCRIPTION OF THE EXISTING STATE OF AFFAIRS
1. DESCRIPTION OF THE EXISTING STATE OF AFFAIRS
2. INTRANET...
COLLECTION OF INFORMATION - INVENTORY OF FUNCTIONAL CONTENT.................................
1. PHOTOS..
2. PRESS SUBSCRIPTION............................
3. MAILING LIST SYSTEM............................
4. GENERAL SEARCH ENGINE......................
5. BREADCRUMB.......................................
6. NEWS AND E DATEBOOK MODULUS ....
7. CONTACT FORM.....................................
8. CONTACT FORM FOR EMPLOYMENT............
9. ARCHIVING SYSTEM...............................
10. "INDUSTRIAL WASTELAND AND DISPOSAL" SECTION
DEVELOPMENT AND PROPOSED SOLUTION.....
GRAPHICAL CHARTER....................................
INFORATION ARCHITECTURE...........................
1. SITE PLAN...
2. CONTENT PLAN ....
ERGONOMICS AND ACCESSIBILITY ....
1. CONTENTS...
2. REALIZATION STAGE..............................
3. PRODUCTION OF TEMPLATES AND GRAPHIC CONTENT
SEO MARKETING AND VISIBILITY.......................
SUMMARY TABLE...

Figure 2.2. *Example of SEO specifications*[1]

---

1 Example of SEO specifications, available at: https://yellowdolphins.com/wp-content/uploads/2015/12/cahier-des-charges.png.

When we receive the customer's specifications, we make a time estimate for each task requested.

If we observe that there are missing elements which are necessary to carry out the project, such as a study of keywords, we are duty bound to mention it, so that the client does not miss out on advice. We define the deadlines with the client and we must mutually respect them to ensure that all integrations related to SEO recommendations are put online on the scheduled dates.

Since SEO results take longer to implement than other channels (such as SEA or SMO), it is essential to keep a reverse schedule and respect it to the letter to ensure that everything is online when planned.

After taking into account the objectives during discussions and possible corrections with the client in relation to the specifications, we can start the support process, which consists initially of holding a kick-off meeting.

2.2. The kick-off meeting

The kick-off meeting is a step that allows SEO consultants and clients to express their needs in order to move forward mutually on the project. It is during this meeting that the client must specify objectives, the key performance indicators (KPIs) to be monitored and what the client expects from their website by optimizing it correctly for search engines.

There are many KPIs to measure and monitor in SEO. Here is an example of some KPIs that we have chosen to use and that we follow to ensure that a website is well optimized in terms of SEO and organic traffic:

– monthly SEO positions;

– unique monthly visits;

– number of page views;

– backlinks;

– remaining 4xx error pages;

– remaining 3xx pages (to be removed);

– bounce rate;

– orphaned/poorly linked pages if necessary;

– page indexing rate (number of real pages in the site versus the number of pages indexed by Google);

– active page rate (i.e. pages that have received at least one SEO visit per month);

– inactive page rate (i.e. pages that have not received any SEO visits per month);

– monthly conversions;

– monthly transactions;

– other KPIs that customers can request on demand.

Following the start-up meeting, where all parties are in agreement, we then set up a reverse schedule to carry out the defined actions.

2.3. Reverse schedules

In order to carry out the optimizations in SEO, we must set up, with the client, a reverse schedule including the dates of realization and deliverables outstanding. For more visibility, we use the Gantt chart model as a basis for the follow-up.

Used in project management, the Gantt chart is one of the most concrete tools for visually representing the progress of the various activities (tasks) that constitute a project. Often, the left column of the diagram lists all the tasks to be performed and the header line represents the most appropriate time units (or dates) for the project (days, weeks, months, etc.). Each task is materialized by a horizontal bar, whose position and length represent the start date, duration and end date.

Figure 2.3 shows an example of the type of Gantt chart we make for our SEO projects.

The Gantt chart is available as a tool and software online[2], but it can also be created in an Excel file using spreadsheets. It is therefore not necessary to invest in software to create a Gantt chart.

───────────────

2 Gantt.com, available at: https://www.gantt.com/.

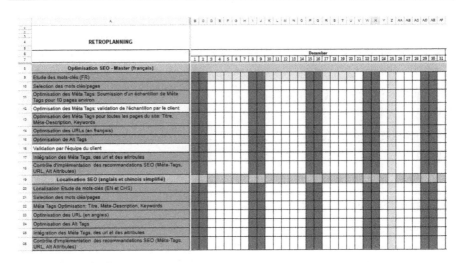

Figure 2.3. *Example of a Gantt chart reverse schedule (in French)*

Following the implementation of a shared reverse schedule and proofreading, correction and validation by the client and external service providers on the web development side, we can start to tackle the concrete steps of the SEOproject, namely technical, semantic and link building audits, as well as keyword studies, meta tags, content, URL and alt attribute optimizations, and finally the implementation and integration of technical recommendations.

2.4. Technical audit of the site

The technical SEO audit phase is one of the pillars of SEO. It is at this stage that we analyze, observe and report on all the issues that prevent search engines from accessing certain web pages of the site (which are often strategic and important for the client). In the technical audit phase, we observe the following elements:

– the crawl of the site;

– indexing of web pages;

– the loading time of the pages;

– internal linking;

– the structure of the site (no significant depths).

The technical audit detects all anomalies that prevent search engine bots from crawling, indexing, referencing and ranking web pages in their search results.

Figure 2.4 provides an overview of an SEO tool dashboard that can detect all anomalies in terms of crawls, URLs that cannot be indexed by engines, etc.

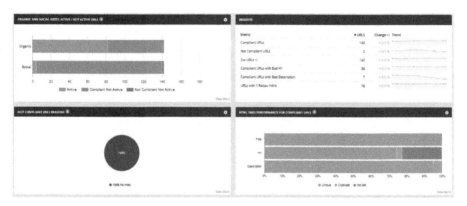

Figure 2.4. *Overview of the dashboard of an SEO tool detecting technical anomalies*

A technical audit deliverable consists of between 30 and 50 pages, depending on the volume of the audited site.

This step is therefore crucial. That is why we will come back to all the technical points on checking and auditing for a website in Chapter 3, which focuses on technical SEO.

2.5. Implementation of technical recommendations

Following the technical audit, we must send our deliverable to the client for validation and, subsequently, send the implementation of our SEO recommendations to the external or internal service providers who develop the website.

The latter must study the feasibility of the recommendations and put in place the advice in order to start sending positive signals of optimization to search engines. This may start by correcting technical files such as robots.

txt, sitemap.xml, the .htaccess file (for page redirections), minimizing JavaScripts or CSS (for loading times to be reduced), setting up missing tracking codes (Google Analytics, Baidu Tongji or Yandex Metrica), etc.

For this purpose, during the technical audit phase, we carry out a technical SEO action plan, which must be regularly monitored and updated by the team of developers (see Figure 2.5).

Action ID	Action	To be done by	Date of completion	Priority	Status
1	Technical audit	SEO consultant	12/09/2018	High	DONE
2	Semantic audit	Rankwell	12/09/2018	High	DONE
3	Clean up 404 pages	Technical team / web developer		High	KO
4	Clean up the 301 and 302 pages on the site	Technical team / web developer		High	KO
5	Reduce home page loading times	Technical team / web developer		High	KO
6	Reduce category page loading times	Technical team / web developer		High	KO
7	Reduce information page loading times	Technical team / web developer		High	KO
8	Outsource .js and .css files so that they are retrievable when loading the site	Technical team / web developer		High	KO

Figure 2.5. *Overview of the technical part of the SEO action plan (in French) with the actions to be carried, by who, the date they should be carried out, priority level and status provided*

Following (or alongside) the implementation of technical actions, the semantic audit can be carried out in order to detect problems related to the existing editorial content and the content to be optimized.

2.6. Semantic audit of the site

During the semantic audit phase, we research the issues related to editorial content in order to understand why the web pages of a site do not pick up enough on various key terms. For this audit, we look at the meta tags (or metadata) that are generally composed of the tags < title> and <meta description>. Metadata can also refer to meta robots, meta itemprop, etc. However, during the semantic audit stage, we focus on the meta *title* tags and meta description.

We also check the editorial titles that are the heading titles HN (most often called H1, H2, H3, etc., in the technical jargon of SEO). These HN tags have a certain semantic influence for SEO and must therefore be used with the right hierarchy in order to have well-ordered pages and structured information (from the most general to the most specific) for Internet users and search engines.

This is also the step where we detect if it is appropriate to set up URL rewriting (rewriting URLs with keywords).

Indeed, if the URLs of the site are composed of parameters, if they are without keywords or if they use underscores as separators, we must propose rewriting. We will come back to this point in Chapter 4 on semantic SEO.

Alt attributes for images should also be checked in this phase to ensure that alternative content describing images is present and optimized for image engines (such as Google Images, Baidu Tupian, i.e. "Baidu Images" in English, Yandex.Images, etc.).

To summarize, in the semantic audit phase, we must audit all content written in the strategic areas of a web page in order to be sure that it can be traced back to high-potential keywords.

In section 2.7, we will discuss the subject of keyword search and explain what this step is all about.

2.7. The study of keywords

During the keyword research phase of a market study of what Internet users in a country are looking for, it is important to keep in mind that this step is part of the strategic starting point for successful SEO. Indeed, if the keywords chosen during this phase generate little interest or research per month or per year, it is preferable to choose other keywords.

To choose the keywords, we must ask ourselves the following questions:

– Has this word been searched for enough?

– Is this word too competitive?

– Does this word match the theme of my page?

– Who positions themselves with regard to this word? (See competitors in search results.)

Keywords are part of SEO's semantic strategy. They are very important to define and target the way a site wants to communicate and position itself.

The study of keywords is also an essential step in an SEO strategy, because it allows you to:

– be aware of how Internet users talk about a theme;

– understand the expectations of Internet users with regard to a subject;

– optimize the website with popular keywords;

– position yourself around sought-after and specific requests for which you want to be a specialist in your niche.

In Chapter 4, we will also return to this part of the keyword study and share our methodology for searching, choosing and organizing keywords.

In the following section, we will explain the optimization of textual content in web pages by "editorial content" (i.e. whether it is articles, product sheets, category descriptions, products, concepts, etc.).

2.8. Content optimization

Content is one of the most important points to work on in SEO. We define the term "content" as "editorial/visual/video content that attracts the interest of Internet users and is easily crawlable and indexable by search engines".

John Mueller, a Google spokesman, shared this point with us: "Do not fill your sites with poor quality content. Instead, work on what will make your sites the best in their field".

With regard to textual content, attention must be paid to the penalties that search engine algorithms can impose (Panda[3] is Google's algorithm against farms with poor quality written content such as automatically generated text, duplicate content; Pomegranate[4], Baidu's algorithm for the same types of problems). Quality content will always be more relevant for websites.

---

3 "Panda, a Google algorithm against content farms", available at: https://en.wikipedia.org/wiki/Google_Panda.

4 "Pomegranate, l'algorithme de Baidu contre les pages de mauvaise qualité ayant des pop-ups, des contenus non informatifs, etc.", available at: https://autoveille.info/2016/01/11/les-algorithms-seo-de-baidu-pomegranate-%e7%9f%b3%e6%a6%b4and-money-plant-%e7%bb%bf%e8%90%9d/.

Content continues to be the best factor in attracting Internet users to a site, as buyers use content to inform their purchasing decisions. In addition, the diversity of content is very important to get people to return to a site.

However, we are now seeing that many companies still consider the creation of texts (or photos/videos) to be a time-consuming task, requiring both imagination and creativity.

Writing quality texts is a time-consuming activity, but it is essential to ensure search engines come back often to crawl and see updates to a site.

2.9. Integration of optimized content

Following the creation of optimized textual content and the production of quality photos and videos, they must be integrated into the site. Integrations must be scheduled in the reverse schedule and be done quickly enough such that search engines can locate updates on the site as quickly as possible and come back to the crawler more often.

The duration of integrations will be variable depending on the volume of the site pages. The larger a site is in terms of page volume, the longer integrations can take. Ideally, for the integration of optimized titles and meta descriptions, we recommend using modules, extensions or even custom tools developed in-house in order to automatically integrate all the elements into the site.

From our point of view, we prefer automatic data integration or import, as this saves a considerable amount of time and reduces the error rate.

Following this phase of integration of technical and semantic recommendations into the site, which we also call "on-site optimizations", we move on to the external part of the site, which consists of auditing the site's external environment (we often talk about referring domains, external links, elements that we can read on social networks, forums, etc.). In SEO, we are mainly interested in referring domains and external links that point to the site. All the elements that affect social networks, forums and specialized sites are more related to *Social Media Optimization*, or the e-reputation of the site, which are two other areas closely related to SEO.

2.10. Auditing of external links

Why should we be interested in the referring domains and external links that point to the site? These domains and links are seen as external quality signals. The more a site has, the more it is considered "popular", with a certain stature and a good reputation.

However, since 2012 and the arrival of the Penguin[5] algorithm, external link farms have been penalized by the Penguin algorithm. Other search engines subsequently developed equivalent algorithms to Penguin. For example, Baidu has created Money Plant[6], an algorithm designed to sanction link farms. Money Plant (绿萝) was launched in February 2013, with the objective of combating spam links and penalizing sites that have link farms. Baidu implemented a disallowance tool in the external link management section of its webmaster tools[7], but as of spring-summer 2015, this tool no longer exists.

Websites with external links that come from low-quality domains can therefore be severely sanctioned by Google, Baidu, Yandex, etc.

This is why it is essential to check a website's external links in order to ensure that the domains referring to the sites are of a high quality. We can check domain names and links in various tools, including Ahrefs, one of the best known SEO tools on the market (see Figure 2.6).

Figure 2.6. *Ahrefs logo, an SEO tool used to check referrer domains and external links*

5 "Penguin, a Google algorithm against bad quality external link farms", available at: https://en.wikipedia.org/wiki/Google_Penguin.
6 "Money Plant de Baidu", available at: https://autoveille.info/2016/01/11/les-algorithmes-seo-de-baidu-pomegranate-%e7%9f%b3%e6%a6%b4-and-money-plant-%e7%bb%bf%e8%90%9d/.
7 "Baidu Webmaster Tools", available at: https://ziyuan.baidu.com/ (in Chinese).

The idea is to collect as many external links as possible, of high quality, on referring sites and media. It is these that constitute the popularity of the website (nearly 50%). It is indeed necessary to do real work on domains and external links in order to position the site based on interesting keywords.

Alongside this phase of optimizing domains and external links, once the technical and semantic integrations are completed, we must check if all the elements are correctly implemented. We then move on to the acceptance phase.

2.11. Technical and semantic acceptance testing

After the integration of the recommendations, we must check the site in order to be sure that all the recommendations have been taken into account. To this end, we usually repeat the audits we carried out at the beginning and look step by step at whether or not the recommendation has been implemented. We have a list of action points in an SEO action plan which we can also use to do the verification.

Figure 2.7 shows an example of acceptance testing for a client case.

Action ID	Action	To be done by	Date of completion	Priority	Status	Comment (in case of obstructive problems, specific requests, etc.)
1	Technical audit	SEO consultant	12/09/2018	High	DONE	
2	Semantic audit	Rankwell	12/09/2018	High	DONE	
3	Clean up 404 pages	Technical team / web developer		High	KO	
4	Clean up the 301 and 302 pages on the site	Technical team / web developer		High	KO	
5	Reduce home page loading times	Technical team / web developer		High	KO	See the Dareboost report in the audit
6	Reduce category page loading times	Technical team / web developer		High	KO	See the Dareboost report in the audit
7	Reduce information page loading times	Technical team / web developer		High	KO	See the Dareboost report in the audit
8	Outsource .js and .css files so that they are retrievable when loading the site	Technical team / web developer		High	KO	
9	Remove the orphaned pages isolated on the site	Technical team / web developer		High	KO	
10	Indexing pages x Faceted navigation [once a choice has been verified, the other links must be put in JS so that search engines do not find them. Otherwise we'll have a multitude of URLs]	Technical team / web developer		High	KO	

Figure 2.7. *SEO action plan for the verification of all implemented actions (in French)*

Below is an example where the initial audit was repeated for the acceptance testing and for which we put our comments in boxes. When the recommendation has been well implemented, we insert a green box with an

OK and possibly a comment, and when the recommendation has not been implemented, we insert a red box also with a comment (see Figure 2.8).

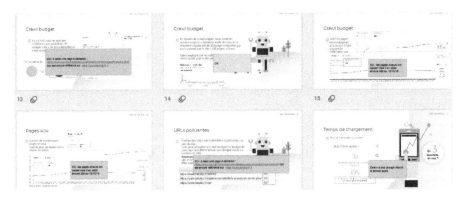

Figure 2.8. *Acceptance testing of technical recommendations and semantics within the SEO audit. For a color version of this figure, see www.iste.co.uk/duong/SEO1.zip*

Following acceptance testing, we send the commented document back to the technical service providers, so that they can reimplement or re-examine the feasibility of the new recommendations we made during the audit.

We repeat the operation with the site owner and technical service providers until the technical and semantic recommendations are fully implemented.

After implementing all the recommendations, it is now possible for us to monitor the evolution of SEO by making monthly or quarterly reports.

2.12. Follow-up, maintenance and reporting

In order to properly monitor the performance of a site following the implementation of SEO technical, semantic and link building recommendations and optimizations, we can start monitoring its evolution via KPIs such as:

– monthly SEO positions;

– unique monthly visits;

– number of page views;

– backlinks;

– remaining 404 error pages;

– remaining 3xx pages (to be removed);

– bounce rate;

– monthly conversions;

– monthly turnover;

– page indexing rate (number of real pages in the site versus the number of pages indexed by search engines).

Traffic performance measurement tools exist for each search engine. Here are the best known, which we use regularly:

– Google Analytics (American);

– Baidu Tongji (Chinese);

– Yandex Metrica (Russian).

These statistical tools indicate visits from different channels or traffic sources (natural, paid, social networks, emails, direct, etc.), unique visits, page views, average time spent per visit, bounce rate, etc.

Figure 2.9 provides an overview of the Google Analytics audience dashboard.

Figure 2.9. *Google Analytics, audience overview in a 7-day, 1-month or 1-year range*

Figure 2.10 provides an overview of Baidu Tongji's audience dashboard.

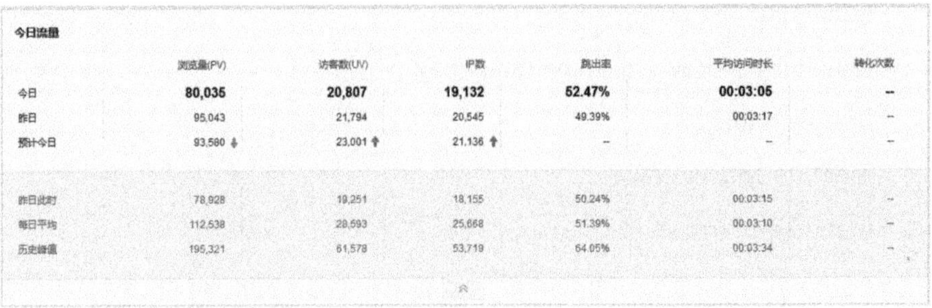

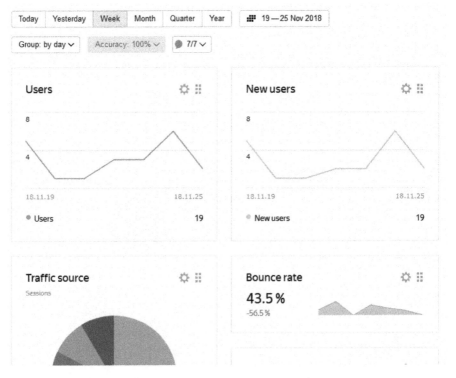

Figure 2.10. *Baidu Tongji, audience overview per day*

Figure 2.11 provides an overview of Yandex Metrica's audience dashboard.

Figure 2.11. *Yandex Metrica, 7-day audience and KPI overview*

We find that each of these analytical tools has its own measurement criteria. For example, in relation to date ranges, some display data on a daily basis, such as Baidu, and others over a period of 7 days to 1 month or more, such as Google and Yandex.

Comparing tool data is a way to be more reliable about the information we collect.

For SEO position tracking, there are several types of tools. The best known is SEMrush for tracking the keywords on which a site is ranked by default (see Figure 2.12).

Figure 2.12. *Monitoring the evolution curve of keywords in SEMrush. For a color version of this figure, see www.iste.co.uk/duong/SEO1.zip*

We also use other tools to track a given list of keywords. There are several tools on the market:

– Advanced Web Ranking;

– SEO Power Suite;

– Ahrefs Rank Tracker;

– Myposeo;

– Ranxplorer;

– Monitorank;

– PRORankTracker.

Figure 2.13 provides an overview of a list of followed keywords (most often from site owners who have selected the terms for the keyword study).

Keyword	Position ↓
agence seo baidu	1
agence seo international paris	1
agence seo international paris	1
agence seo international paris	1
agence seo 75017	1
agence seo internationale paris	1
agence référencement international paris	1 ▲ 39
agence seo baidu	1
agence seo google	1 ▲ 1
agence seo 75017	1

Figure 2.13. *Ahrefs Rank Tracker (in French)*

Managing an SEO project requires a lot of organization, rigor and follow-ups. During SEO support, we have to face various problems and it often happens that there are unforeseen events (a peak of pages "404 errors", problems with indexing new pages, redirections that do not work, late content deliveries, etc.).

As a result, the reverse schedule and the SEO action plan are modified regularly, according to which actions can be postponed.

The SEO field is comprehensive and involves numerous different actors because it highlights various aspects: technical, editorial, web writing, marketing, photo and video optimization, etc.

In Chapter 3, we will discuss the technical points of SEO in detail (crawl budget, redirection plan, internal linking structuration plan, page management, etc.).

3

Technical SEO: from HTML Tags to URL

The technical aspect of SEO takes place in several steps and consists of checking the following points:

– the crawl of the site;

– indexing of web pages;

– the loading time of the pages;

– the internal linking;

– the structure of the site (not too deep).

Here, we provide explanation of these different elements as follows:

– *crawl*: when arriving on a website, search engines look first at the robots.txt to see if they can visit (or crawl) everything on a site. If there are any restrictions, the engines skip the restricted folders and go directly to the authorized folders;

– *indexing*: after entering the various authorized folders, search engines will search for the pages to visit, and then save (index) them in their databases. The sitemap.xml helps to index a site faster;

– *loading time*: the longer it takes for a page to load, the harder it will be to get it out in the search results of the engines. We must be careful at this point, because with the arrival of the new Google and Baidu projects, namely Accelerated Mobile Pages (AMP) and Mobile Instant Pages (MIP), the mobile versions of the sites will be more important than the traditional versions on computer;

– internal linking: a web page can be indexed more quickly if it is easily found in the site structure. The internal linking has a significant impact on the ranking of pages in search engines.

In a technical audit, we check all the points related to the crawl of the site, its indexing, its internal linking, error pages, redirected pages present, loading times (by detecting the most resource-consuming data), page structures, etc.

In order to make the following instructions as concrete as possible and feasible for any consultant looking for a methodology, we will present the whole of the current chapter as a technical audit.

3.1. Simulation of Google's transition

We simulated a search engine visit to a hypothetical site studied. This is called a "crawl" (by a mobile bot in the following case, see Figure 3.1).

This test allows us to identify all the URLs of the site and to have an overview of the site.

It also allows us to fully understand what search engines will face when they visit a site.

Crawl settings default ▾	
Start URL	https://
Crawl limits	Crawl up to *2,500 urls* or up to depth *15*
Crawl bot	Crawl as *Mobile bot* with name *OnCrawl*.

Figure 3.1. *Crawl simulation with a crawl tool like OnCrawl*

Following crawl simulation, we identify a number of URLs. In this case, we have a sample of 1,428 URLs. In the following section, we will see how many URLs comply with the rules of search engines of all types (Google, Baidu, Yandex, Naver, Yahoo! Japan, etc.).

3.2. Compliant URLs for SEO

Of the 1,428 network URLs within the site, 24.9% of them do not have indexing potential. A URL is considered "non-compliant" when it does not meet the following criteria:

– presence of an html page (it must not be script or image files or Flash);

– presence of an HTTP 200 header (no 3xx redirection or 4xx error);

– presence of a canonical tag pointing toward itself (or not indicated);

– absence of meta noindex tags in strategic pages.

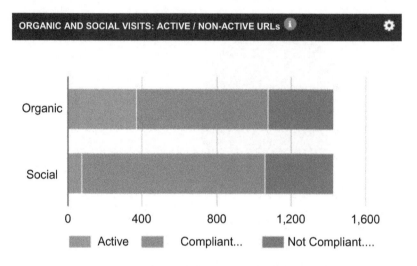

Figure 3.2. *Overview of 1,428 URLs with Botify. For a color version of this figure, see www.iste.co.uk/duong/SEO1.zip*

There are several reasons why URLs do not comply with search engine rules.

3.3. Reasons for non-compliant URLs

At this stage of the audit, we investigate why these URLs do not comply with Google, Baidu, Yandex, etc., guidelines.

After several searches, it appears that a large majority of URLs do not have indexing potential for several reasons:

– they have a "noindex" meta tag instruction (which instructs search engines not to index pages in their databases);

– they are not in HTTP code 200 (97.3%), which means that these pages respond in code 3xx (redirection), 4xx (error detected in the request sent by the client to the server) or 5xx (code indicating that the client's request seemed correct, but that an error was detected when it was processed by the server).

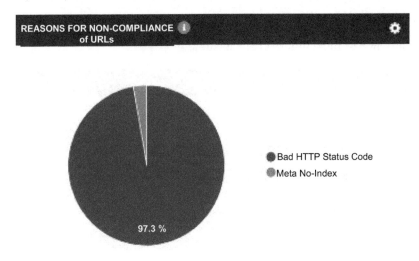

Figure 3.3. *Graph showing the reasons for URL non-compliance (tool used: Botify)*

After detecting the reasons why URLs are not indexed within a site, we can look at the number of active pages (i.e. pages that receive at least one visit from organic/SEO traffic per month) versus inactive pages (which do not receive any monthly visits from SEO).

3.4. Active versus inactive pages

In our current case, the majority of web pages are not active within the site and these can be the strategic pages.

When we analyze the situation more closely, inactive pages are often those that are either at significant depth levels in the site (beyond three clicks, a page is difficult for an Internet user or a search engine to access), or poor in terms of content.

In the case studied, few pages are active: only 4.5% receive at least one organic/SEO visit per month.

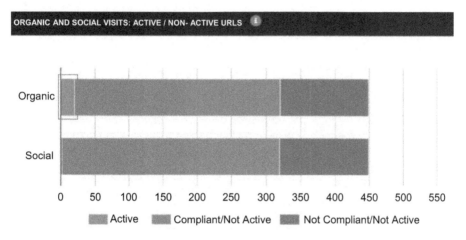

Figure 3.4. *Rate of active versus inactive pages in the case studied (tool used: Botify). For a color version of this figure, see www.iste.co.uk/duong/SEO1.zip*

In our example, which seems to be the general case on most sites, the problem with the inactive pages is that the URLs are deeply linked within the site. We will analyze this issue in the next section.

3.5. Active and inactive pages × depth

Some interesting pages that are too deep receive very few SEO visits per month. They should be redesigned as close as possible to the home page, so that they receive more visits.

Inactive pages are composed of pages without SEO visits over a month. These pages should be further promoted (e.g. by making a selection) and the content rewritten, i.e. made more attractive and informative for users.

The main problem in our case concerns the product pages (catalogues) of the site. Indeed, the catalogues are meshed in depth 9 for the majority and therefore do not generate any SEO visits per month.

Our recommendation is that it is absolutely necessary to rethink the page format, create HTML pages and network them higher up in the site structure.

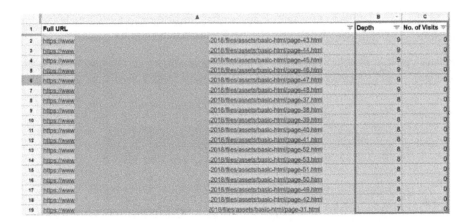

Figure 3.5. *Detection and analysis of deep pages within a site not generating any SEO visits per month*

After finding the reason why some pages do not generate SEO visits per month, we focus on analyzing the crawl budget of the site.

3.6. Crawl budget of a site

The crawl budget is the URL budget allocated by search engines for each site. For a site of 1,500 pages, an engine can allocate only 500 URLs. It is then necessary to show 500 relevant pages to the crawlers, so that they index the best pages or new pages, and make them position themselves as quickly as possible in the search results. In the case below, we took a site with 449 mesh URLs. To observe a site's crawl budget, we can use Google's Search Console, Ziyuan Baidu (tools for webmasters for the Chinese engine) or Yandex Webmaster. The site's Apache log files also provide a wealth of information to detect and help understand how engine robots pass and visit the URLs of a site.

With Google's Search Console, we take our case from the site with 449 mesh URLs. Once we analyze the crawl budget, we realize that we are above the actual volume of the site, since the average allocated is 211 pages explored per day. Knowing that the site has 449 pages, some of them are never crawled by Google.

Crawl Stats

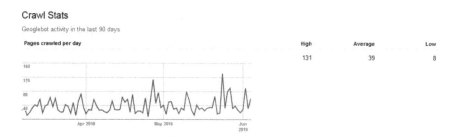

Figure 3.6. *Site crawl statistics in Google Search Console*

When we notice that half of the pages of the site are not crawled and indexed by search engines, we analyze them in order to understand why. In most cases, we are dealing with polluting URLs.

3.7. Polluting URLs

When there are non-indexable and polluting URLs within the site, these can disrupt the crawl budget (which refers to the time Google spends on site links). Our recommendation is to remove polluting URLs (error pages or redirection pages), i.e. remove them from the site structure's network, and then replace them with URLs to which they are redirected. Often the polluting URLs are 404 (pages that no longer exist), 301 (pages that are permanently redirected and transmit the popularity of the old page to the new one) or 302 (pages that are temporarily redirected, which would not transmit the popularity or link juice from the old page to the new URL).

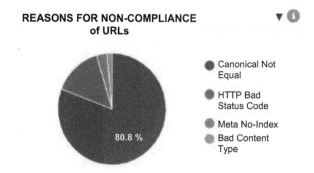

Figure 3.7. *Reasons for URLs that do not comply with search engines and pollute the crawl budget. For a color version of this figure, see www.iste.co.uk/duong/SEO1.zip*

Ideally, a site should have a 100% rate of pages responding in code 200 (i.e. existing pages and return content), with an HTML format, without noindex or canonical tags, so that search engine robots visit as many pages as possible within the site.

Following the study of the crawl budget, we check the points relating to page loading times. We also detect if alternative pages in AMP (Google), MIP (Baidu) and Turbo Pages (Yandex) exist for mobile versions.

3.8. The objectives of AMP, MIP and Turbo Pages

In 2015, Google launched the AMP project with the aim of accelerating the loading time of mobile web pages as quickly as possible. In 2016 and 2017, Baidu and Yandex launched their own versions: MIP and Turbo Pages.

For all engines, it should be noted that they prefer classic sites in Responsive Design, which can be adapted to all screens (computers, mobiles, tablets, TV, etc.). Because of Responsive Design, there is only one version of the site to crawl, index and position.

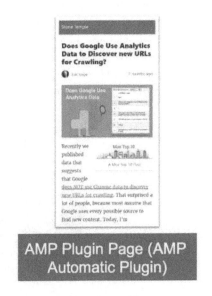

Figure 3.8. *A mobile page in Responsive Design versus an AMP page (there are fewer graphic elements on the latter)*

Nevertheless, with AMP, MIP and Turbo Pages, we need to create a new alternative mobile version that is even subtler than Responsive Design.

Here are the objectives of Google's AMP project:

– allow only asynchronous scripts: to prevent JavaScript from delaying page rendering, AMP only allows asynchronous JavaScript scripts;

– prevent extension mechanisms from blocking rendering: AMP prevents extension mechanisms from blocking page rendering. AMP supports extensions of objects such as mosaics, Instagram integrations, tweets, etc.;

– remove third-party JavaScript from the main process;

– all CSS style must be online and limited in size: in AMP HTML pages, only online styles are allowed. The size of online style sheets is limited to a maximum of 50 KB.

Here, we provide recommendations for companies wishing to have an alternative version of a website in AMP (or MIP or Turbo Pages): it is necessary to create a version identical to the main pages of the site and code the duplicated versions of the pages with the AMP HTML code presented in Figure 3.9.

```
 1  <!DOCTYPE html>
 2  <html ⚡ lang="fr">
 3  <head>
 4    <meta charset="utf-8">
 5    <meta name="viewport" content="width=device-width,minimum-scale=1,initial-scale=1">
 6    <meta property="og:description" content="The Accelerated Mobile Pages (AMP) Project
 7    <meta property="og:image" content="https://www.ampproject.org/static/img/logo-og-ima
 8    <meta name="description" content="The Accelerated Mobile Pages (AMP) Project is an ope
 9    <meta name="google-site-verification" content="DPQFQ0Loo-Qiz2pYWfboqYb03QnnVUMb0RDvq
10    <meta name="amp-google-client-id-api" content="googleanalytics">
11    <script type="application/ld+json">
12    {
13      "@context": "http://schema.org",
14      "@type": "Webpage",
15      "url": "https://www.ampproject.org/fr/",
16      "name": "AMP Project",
17      "headline":"Accelerated Mobile Pages Project",
18      "description":"The Accelerated Mobile Pages (AMP) Project is an open source initia
19      "mainEntityOfPage": {
20        "@type": "WebPage",
21        "@id": "https://www.ampproject.org/fr/"
22      },
23      "publisher": {
24        "@type": "Organization",
25        "name": "AMP Project",
26        "logo": {
27          "url": "https://www.ampproject.org/assets/img/logo-blue.svg",
28          "width": 175,
29          "height": 60,
30          "@type": "ImageObject"
31        }
```

Figure 3.9. *Example of HTML AMP source code (Google)*

To check if a page is AMP friendly, we can pass it through the AMP Validator[1] tool, as shown in Figure 3.10.

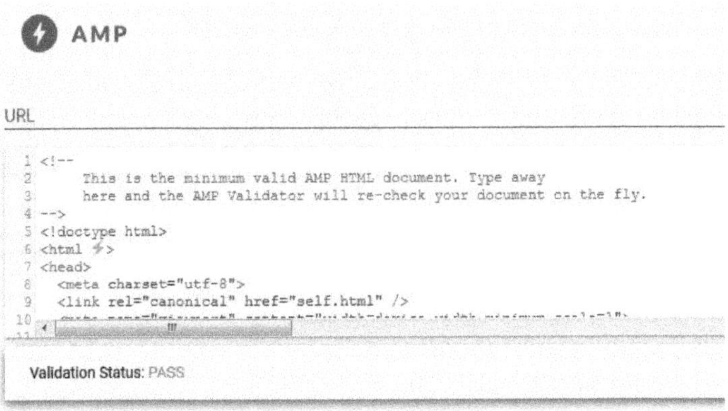

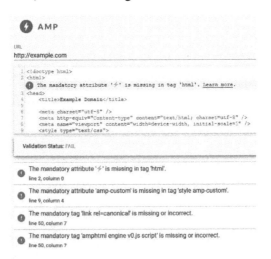

Figure 3.10. *Validation of AMP pages with the AMP Validator tool*

If the page is AMP friendly, we have the status "PASS" which is displayed in green. Otherwise, we have a message and the errors that are mentioned in the tool, as shown in Figure 3.11.

Figure 3.11. *Example of a non-AMP-friendly page, with the problem points reported*

1 "AMP Validator", available at: https://validator.ampproject.org; https://validator.Amp project.org/.

AMP and other versions such as MIP and Turbo Pages are now part of the HTML and XML languages to be used to create alternative mobile websites that meet current and future uses in terms of mobile-compatible sites.

Search engines recommend having pages that load in 3 seconds maximum on mobile phones, and even in 3G connection. By 2020, it is estimated that many countries will be connected to 3G, according to the Think with Google tool (see Figure 3.12).

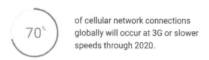

Figure 3.12. *Think with Google indicates that 70% of mobile connections will be 3G, or even 2G, in 2020*

To optimize page loading times, we also audit page types to ensure that all pages on the site are fast enough on the Web. In the following section, we present a case study on the analysis of problem points for web page loading times.

3.9. Loading times by page type

To measure and analyze page loading times, we divide a site by page type:

– home page;

– category pages;

– sub-category pages;

– product or article pages.

We run the pages in load time measurement tools such as Dareboost or Web Page Test, then we obtain the average load time of the pages in a specific country and on a mobile or browser model.

In addition to the load times, we also take into account the speed index. This metric can be defined as the average time it takes for each visible part of a page to be displayed. It is expressed in milliseconds and depends on the device on which the test is performed (PC, iPhone 6, Samsung Galaxy S6, etc.). The speed index metric was created in 2012 and measures the loading time of the contents of a page (the smaller the score, the better). The speed index is particularly useful for comparing user experiences (before/after optimization, a site versus its competitors, etc.) and should be combined with other metrics such as load time or start render in order to better understand site performance.

It should also be noted that the speed index is a score measuring the time it takes for content to appear above the fold.

What is a good speed index? A good speed index (on mobile) is below 3,000. Here is what the score ranges mean:

– very good: less than 2,000;

– good: less than 3,000;

– fair: less than 5,000;

– bad: between 5,000 and 10,000;

– very bad: more than 10,000.

On a computer, it is recommended to have a speed index equal to or less than 1,000.

Figure 3.13 provides an example of a homepage that has a long loading time and a speed index above 3,000.

Figure 3.13. *Simulation of an iPhone 6S visit in Paris on a homepage loading over more than 10 seconds with a speed index higher than 3,000. For a color version of this figure, see www.iste.co.uk/duong/SEO1.zip*

Often, the home pages of Western sites are faster than Asian sites, as the latter have many banners, links and information. Mobile loading time performance measurement tools give reasons and recommendations for optimizing and reducing load times, such as Google Page Speed (see Figure 3.14).

Opportunities – These optimizations can speed up your page load.

Opportunity	Estimated Savings
▦ Defer offscreen images	▬▬▬ 0.3 s ⌄
▦ Serve images in next-gen formats	▬▬▬ 0.3 s ⌄
▦ Eliminate render-blocking resources	▬▬ 0.18 s ⌄
▦ Enable text compression	▬▬ 0.15 s ⌄

Figure 3.14. *Google Speed Insights gives ideas for optimizations to speed up the loading time of web pages*

For all search engines, the loading times of a website have become real criteria for ranking. The faster a site loads, the more likely it is to stand out better in search results, and therefore to position itself correctly in them. Figure 3.15 provides a histogram showing the correlation between a fast loading time and the positioning of pages in engines.

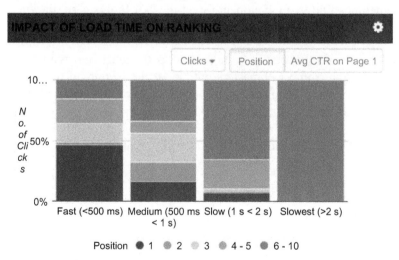

Figure 3.15. *Correlation of loading time x SEO positions. For a color version of this figure, see www.iste.co.uk/duong/SEO1.zip*

With the graph in Figure 3.15, we can clearly see that the faster a page loads on a computer and/or mobile, the better it is positioned in Google's search results.

We also notice in the graph that pages that load in less than 500 msec are mostly positioned in position 1 in Google. There is therefore a correlation between loading times and page ranking in search engines.

In the next section, we will explain what robots.txt is and why it is important to optimize it correctly for crawlers.

3.10. Robots.txt

When they arrive on a website, search engines look first at the robots.txt to see if they can visit (or crawl) everything on that site.

If there are restrictions (disallow), the engines skip the restricted folders and go directly to the authorized folders.

Restrictions or permissions with errors will not be taken into account by search engine robots.

The file "robots.txt" is always written with an "s" at the end of "robots". We sometimes find that developers forget the "s". In this case, the file is no longer considered valid and search engines may therefore have to ignore it.

The syntax of robots.txt is quite precise: paths must start with a "/". We also observe that some webmasters put "*" at the beginning of the path in the file. However, it should be noted that the robots.txt does not take into account the wildcard characters "*" like for regular expressions (regex) at the beginning of the path and the asterisk is only valid for the user-agent or certain other cases mentioned below (see the explanation of the directive below).

Here is the syntax proposed by Google (also valid for other search engines) in its online documentation[2]:

---

2 "Complete Google documentation on robots.txt", available at: https://support.google.com/webmasters/answer/6062596?hl=en.

– the robots.txt file must be an ASCII or UTF-8 text file. No other characters are allowed;

– a robots.txt file consists of one or more rules;

– each rule is composed of several directives (instructions) and only one directive per line is required.

A rule provides the following information:

– the robot (user-agent) to which the rule applies;

– the directories or files which this agent can access, if applicable;

– the directories or files which this agent cannot access, if applicable;

– rules are treated from top to bottom and the same user-agent can only fall under one rule, defined as the first most specific rule governing his behavior;

– the starting principle is that from the moment a page or directory is not blocked by a disallow rule, the user-agent can explore it;

– the rules are case sensitive[3].

The following directives are used in robots.txt files:

– *user-agent* (mandatory, one or more per rule): refers to the search engine robot (exploration robot software) to which the rule applies. This is the first line of any rule. Most user-agent names are listed in the web robot database or in the Google list of user-agents. It is compatible with the wildcard character "*" for a prefix, suffix or complete path string. The use of an asterisk (*), as in the example below, allows all exploration robots to be included, with the exception of the various AdsBot exploration robots, which must be explicitly named. Here, we have some examples:

> # Example 1: Only block Googlebot
> User-agent: Googlebot
> Disallow: /
>
> # Example 2: Block Googlebot and Adsbot
> User-agent: Googlebot
> User-agent: AdsBot-Google
> Disallow: /

---

3 For example, disallow: /fichier.asp applies to http://www.example.com/fichier.asp, but not to http://www.example.com/Fichier.asp.

```
# Example 3: Block all bots
User-agent: *
Disallow: /
```

– *disallow* (at least one or more disallow or allow entries per rule): refers to the directory or page, related to the root domain, that must not be explored by the user-agent. For a page, it must be the full name of the page, as indicated in the browser. For a directory, the name must end with a slash (/). It is compatible with the wildcard character "*" for a prefix, suffix or complete path string;

– *allow* (at least one or more disallow or allow entries per rule): refers to the directory or page, related to the root domain, that must be explored by the user-agent mentioned above. This directive is used to bypass the disallow instruction applied to a directory and allow the exploration of one of its pages or subdirectories. For a page, it must be the full name of the page, as indicated in the browser. For a directory, the name must end with a slash (/). It is compatible with the wildcard character "*" for a prefix, suffix or complete path string;

– *sitemap* (optional, zero or more per file): refers to the location of a sitemap for this website. The URL provided must be complete. Google does not deduce variants (http, https, www, non-www, etc.) or check them. Sitemaps are a good way to indicate what content Google should explore, as opposed to content that it can or cannot explore. You can discover more about sitemaps[4]. Note that unknown keywords are ignored.

Figure 3.16 shows an example of a robots.txt with restriction and permission instructions.

The relevance of the pages or directories to be blocked or not in a robots.txt depends on the site owner's evaluation. For some owners, the legal notices must be crawled and indexed by the engines and, for others, they consider that these pages are not strategic and can be blocked in the robots.txt in order to give way to more strategic pages such as categories pages, products, articles, etc.

---

4 Example of sitemaps: https://example.com/sitemap.xml; http://www.example.com/sitemap.xml.

```
Sitemap: https://autoveille.info/sitemap.xml
Sitemap: https://autoveille.info/news-sitemap.xml

User-agent: *
Disallow: /wp-admin/
Allow: /wp-admin/admin-ajax.php
Disallow: /wp-login.php
Disallow: /activate/ # har har
Disallow: /cgi-bin/ # MT refugees
Disallow: /mshots/v1/
Disallow: /next/
Disallow: /public.api/

User-agent: IRLbot
Crawl-delay: 3600

# This file was generated on Mon, 09 Apr 2018 23:16:53 +0000
```

Figure 3.16. *Robots.txt from the blog autoveille.info*

After processing the robots.txt, we can optimize the sitemap.xml, which is a sitemap for search engine crawlers.

3.11. Sitemap.xml

After entering the various folders and pages allowed in robots.txt, search engines will search for pages to visit and then index in their databases.

The sitemap.xml helps to index a site faster. We recommend the following hierarchy to prioritize (in the <priority> tags of a sitemap) the indexing of pages in a site:

– home page: 1.0;

– category pages: 0.8;

– main product pages, bestsellers: 0.8;

– other product pages (ranges, secondary, etc.) : 0.7;

– other pages (company history, team, etc.): 0.5;

– legal pages (legal notices, terms and conditions, etc.): 0.2.

We also recommend having the tag <changefreq> for the frequency of page changes and to indicate the following elements for the types of pages concerned:

– home page: daily;

– news pages (blog, magazine, news, etc.): daily;

– category pages: weekly;

– product pages: daily;

– legal notices, terms and conditions, etc.: monthly.

Here, we present the complete Google documentation for creating a sitemap.xml and sending it to Webmaster Tools (Search Console for Google, Ziyuan for Baidu, Yandex Webmaster for Yandex, Naver Webmaster Tools for Naver, etc.):

– use consistent and absolute URLs: search engines visit URLs as per the letters. For example, if the site is located on http://www.example.com/, do not specify for the URL /http://example.com/ (without www) or ./ mypage. html (a relative URL);

– do not include a session ID in the URLs of your sitemap to limit the double exploration of these URLs;

– report versions of a URL in another language using hreflang annotations (valid for Google and Yandex);

– sitemap files must be encoded in UTF-8 and URLs must use the appropriate escape characters;

– split large sitemaps into several small sitemaps to prevent the server from being overloaded. A sitemap file cannot contain more than 50,000 URLs and its size must not exceed 10 MB before compression;

– use a sitemap index file to list all individual sitemaps and send this single file, instead of sending each small sitemap separately;

– use sitemap extensions to refer to other types of media, such as videos, images and news.

If you have different URLs for the classic version and the mobile version of a page, we recommend that you refer to only one version. However, if it is necessary to refer to both URLs, the URLs must be annotated to indicate the classic and mobile versions.

If you have other pages for different languages or regions, it is relevant to use the hreflang tags to indicate these URLs.

We recommend using a UTF-8 encoding for the sitemap file. This setting can be set when saving the file.

As with all XML files, data values (including URLs) must use escape codes for the characters listed below.

A sitemap can only contain ASCII characters. It cannot contain ASCII characters in upper case or some control codes or special characters, such as the asterisk (*) and brackets ({}).

If the URL of the sitemap contains the characters in Figure 3.17, an error will be generated when indexing is requested.

Special character	escaped form	gets replaced by
Ampersand	&amp;	&
Less-than	&lt;	<
Greater-than	&gt;	>
Quotes	&quot;	"
Apostrophe	&apos;	'

Figure 3.17. *Special characters and escape codes*

In addition, all URLs (including those of the sitemap) must be encoded in such a way that they can be read by the web server on which they are located and must use the necessary escape characters.

However, if there is any script, tool or log file used to generate URLs (rather than entering them manually), this formatting is usually automatic.

If an error message is returned when sending the sitemap and it indicates that not all URLs can be found, it is necessary to check that the URLs comply with the RFC-3986 standard[5] for URIs, the RFC-3987 standard[6] for IRIs and the XML standard.

---

5 "Uniform Resource Identifier (URI): Generic Syntax 3986", available at: https://tools.ietf.org/html/rfc3986.

6 "Internationalized Resource Identifiers (IRIs) 3987", available at: https://www.ietf.org/rfc/rfc3987.txt.

Figure 3.18. *Sitemap submission via Google Search Console*

To send a sitemap to search engines, there are several ways or methods. We recommend the method that we think is the most efficient and simple to implement (even for people without a technical profile): submit the sitemap(s) in the interfaces of the tools for webmasters such as the Search Console, Yandex Webmaster, Ziyuan Baidu, etc. In Yandex Webmaster, we have a simple interface, and we can easily add our sitemap because of the field presented in Figure 3.19.

Figure 3.19. *Sitemap submission in Yandex Webmaster*

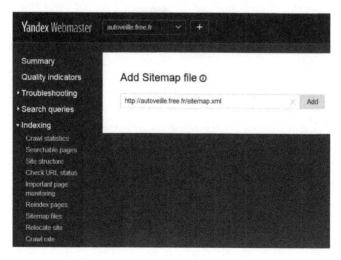

Figure 3.20. *Adding the sitemap.xml of the site in Yandex Webmaster*

We paste the URL of the sitemap.xml into the field and click on the yellow "Add" button (see Figure 3.20).

Then, Yandex tells us that the sitemap is being processed (see Figure 3.21).

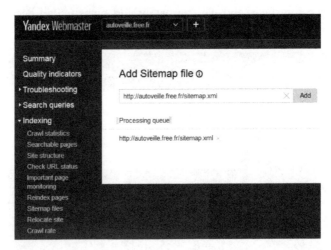

Figure 3.21. *Adding in progress with a "Processing queue" message*

Figure 3.22. *Submission of a sitemap.xml to Baidu Ziyuan*

For Baidu Ziyuan, the location to submit a sitemap.xml is in the menu "数据引入 > 链接提交" (data indexing > URL submission) and you must click on the tab "自动提交" (automatic submission), then on "sitemap" to access it (see Figure 3.21).

Subtly for Baidu, the validation captcha is in Chinese and it is therefore necessary to know how to type in simplified Chinese to finalize the procedure (see Figure 3.23).

Figure 3.23. *Captcha in Chinese to validate the submission of sitemap.xml in Baidu Ziyuan*

Once the verification by captcha has been validated, we can see the submission status. Figure 3.24 shows that we have successfully submitted the sitemap.xml submission step in Baidu.

Following the submission of sitemaps in the various search engines or in the one to be worked on (because the site is monolingual or only concerns one country), we can study the site at a deeper level, namely the 404 error pages to redirect, then the 3xx redirected pages to remove from the site network, and finally the pages with a different canonical tag to see if they are really problematic or not.

文件名称	状态 ▾	提取url数量	最后抓取时间
http://autovelle.free.fr/sitemap.xml	⊘正常	26	2018-12-02 21:16:49
autovelle.free.fr/sitemap.xml	⊘正常	26	2018-11-30 16:46:36

全选   ↻ 手动更新文件   🗑 删除

共2条 每页显示： 10 ▾

Figure 3.24. *Successful submission of the sitemap.xml in Baidu*

3.12. 404 pages

In the lifecycle of a site, several steps are present: the creation of a web page that responds in 200, offering a product, may, over time, reach a stock shortage causing the page to no longer exist, and thus generating error 404 pages. Most of the time, developers or webmasters redirect 302 or 301 errors to other pages, but the work is not finished.

When we have a lot of 404 pages, we set up a redirection plan, in which we point the error pages to existing pages in the site.

To do this, we have a specific method that consists of the following steps:

– crawling the entire site in order to forward all the URLs of the site;

– sorting URLs in order to keep only 404 pages;

– proposal of a URL that will replace the page that no longer exists and that answers the 404;

– setting up all the redirection rules in the file .htaccess or, failing that, in the file httpd.conf (this step is processed by a web developer).

Figure 3.25 shows an example of a redirection plan that we have put in place.

Following these redirections, there are many 301, 302, etc. pages which are generated and, as we have seen previously, pages other than those responding in 200 do not comply with the rules of search engines and are therefore not indexable by them.

We must therefore remove from the network the pages corresponding to 301, 302, etc. We propose a removal method in the following section.

URL	Code de réponse	Redirection 301 sur :
https://www.rankwell.fr/teams/Direct-Method_1351.html	404	https://www.rankwell.fr/blog/
https://www.rankwell.fr/competitions/Dirt-Masters-International_210.html	404	https://www.rankwell.fr/blog/
https://www.rankwell.fr/players/KarjeN_203.html	404	https://www.rankwell.fr/blog/
https://www.rankwell.fr/2013/01/letrange-mais-fascinent-univers-de.html	404	https://www.rankwell.fr/blog/
https://www.rankwell.fr/2013/03/apps-of-love.html	404	https://www.rankwell.fr/blog/
https://www.rankwell.fr/players/Whisper_1115.html	404	https://www.rankwell.fr/blog/
https://www.rankwell.fr/2013/01/oh-my-god-jai-un-entretien-dembauche.html	404	https://www.rankwell.fr/blog/
https://www.rankwell.fr/p/look.html	404	https://www.rankwell.fr/blog/
https://www.rankwell.fr/2012/12/ddj-let-body.html	404	https://www.rankwell.fr/blog/
https://www.rankwell.fr/2013/08/les-jeudi-vesti-orange-is-new-black.html	404	https://www.rankwell.fr/blog/
https://www.rankwell.fr/2013/11	404	https://www.rankwell.fr/blog/
https://www.rankwell.fr/teams/A-New-Era_623.html	404	https://www.rankwell.fr/blog/
https://www.rankwell.fr/2014/11/w-n-d-e-r-l-u-s-t.html	404	https://www.rankwell.fr/blog/
https://www.rankwell.fr/players/Gamble_284.html	404	https://www.rankwell.fr/blog/
https://www.rankwell.fr/competitions/Des-Bois-Competition-6_211.html	404	https://www.rankwell.fr/blog/
https://www.rankwell.fr/players/Akbalder_3824.html	404	https://www.rankwell.fr/blog/
https://www.rankwell.fr/competitions/ESL_ru-Again-Cup-Final_1237.html	404	https://www.rankwell.fr/blog/
https://www.rankwell.fr/2013/03/ddj-la-creme-bienfaisante.html	404	https://www.rankwell.fr/blog/
https://www.rankwell.fr/2014/09/style-of-day-mom-jeans.html	404	https://www.rankwell.fr/blog/

Figure 3.25. *Example of a redirection plan from 404 pages to 200 pages (in French) with response codes and 301 redirection*

3.13. 301/302 redirection

The 301 and 302 pages are ones that no longer exist and have been redirected. Thus, they respond under rescodes 301 and 302, which are the most common redirection rescodes we find in SEO.

These pages must not be linked to the site's network, as they are not indexed by the engines and can disrupt the site's crawl. This is why they should be removed as soon as possible from the site in order to show only healthy URLs (responding in 200, in HTML, etc.) to search engines.

Figure 3.26 illustrates the distribution of pages in 200, 301, 302 and 404 that we regularly see on a site.

The ideal is to find a site with only pages in 200 and without pages in error or pages in redirection, because they disrupt crawlers and Internet users' navigation.

Our recommendation to manage the page lifecycle, including products by season or seasonality (sales, Christmas, Valentine's Day, etc.), is to follow our procedure, which is either to leave the page in 200 (even if the product no longer exists) or to redirect it in 301 (to keep the existing link juice) to a page in 200.

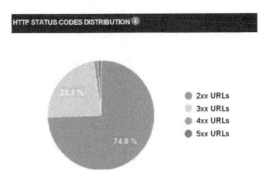

Figure 3.26. *Distribution of pages by rescode within a site. For a color version of this figure, see www.iste.co.uk/duong/SEO1.zip*

To manage the products, we offer two solutions:

1) leave product pages that no longer have stock in 200 (because if they are disabled in the content management system (CMS), they can generate 404 errors);

2) redirect product pages without stock to the parent category page (in 301).

If the first option is chosen, it is necessary to have relevant content on the pages in order to prevent them from being present only for information purposes, and to have a space with similar products to offer.

In the case of the second solution chosen, it should be noted that each redirection adds about 300–500 msec to the loading time of a page. It is therefore necessary to think carefully about optimizing the time it takes to display pages on mobile phones and PCs.

Another point is to avoid cascading redirections (i.e. from page A to page B, then from page B to page C), as search engines have difficulty tracking and understanding the routing.

To clean up internal broken and redirected URLs, we rely on common market referencing tools.

3.14. Removal of broken and redirected URLs

In cases where a redirection plan has been put in place to redirect 404 pages to existing pages, the error pages become redirected pages under rescodes 301 and 302.

Removing 301 and 302 pages from the internal linking, in a small site, is possible to do manually.

Here are the concrete steps for removing the broken links in the internal structure of a website:

1) we go into the HTML source code of pages that still refer to error and/or redirection pages;

2) we identify the link that no longer exists or that is redirected;

3) we remove it from the tag <a href="">;

4) we replace the old redirected URL with the new URL that answers in 200;

5) we save the HTML file;

6) then we send the HTML file to the FTP server in order to put the updated and corrected reference page back online.

Figure 3.27 shows a case study with 301 pages on a website.

URL Card		HTTP Status Code
https:/	/content/21-notice-iphone-reconditionne ☑ </>	301
https:/	/content/10-conditions-generales ☑ </>	301
https:/	/content/11-mangopay ☑ </>	301
https:/	/content/12-certi30 ☑ </>	301
https:/	/content/14-detox ☑ </>	301

Figure 3.27. *301 pages within a site*

We take the first URL and find that it is not indexed by search engines (see Figure 3.28).

MAIN DATA

Date Crawled	2018-10-03 16:49:00
Is Compliant	No
Zone	notset,https
Internal Pagerank	9.5
Internal Pagerank Position	39
Delay Total	302 ms
Content Byte Size	269
HTTP Status Code	301
Depth	1

Figure 3.28. *Status of a URL detailed in 301 that is not compliant and therefore not indexable by search engines*

In our tool, we add the column of pages that reference or link 301 and 302 pages (see Figure 3.29).

Figure 3.29. *Grid removal plan indicating the reference pages that still network the 301 and 302 redirected pages in their HTML source code*

In practice, it is necessary to go to the HTML source codes of the reference pages, locate the link in 301, remove it and replace it with the new URL, which responds in 200.

For example, if we always use the first URL in the table, we go to one of the reference pages (including the one that ends with "comment acheter"), then we open the source code and copy and paste the URL into 301, to see if we find it in the HTML code. It turns out that we find it well networked in the HTML code of the reference page, as confirmed in Figure 3.30.

Figure 3.30. *Reference page still linking the URL to 301 (in French). For a color version of this figure, see www.iste.co.uk/duong/SEO1.zip*

The URL of the pink area in Figure 3.30 must then be replaced by the URL to which it has been redirected. In our case, this is the URL framed in green in Figure 3.31.

URL Card	HTTP Status Code	Sample of Internal Inlinks	Redirect To - Full URL
https://...content/21-notice-iphone-recondtionne ☑ </>	301	• follow https... ☑ </> • follow https... /comment-acheter ☑ </> • follow https... /rachatimmediat ☑ </> • follow https... /iphone-reconditionnes-82 ☑ </> • follow https... /iphone-7-plus-169 ☑ </>	https://...content/21-notice-iphone-reconditionnes ☑ </>

Figure 3.31. *URL in the green box responding in 200, which should replace the URL in 301 in the reference page. For a color version of this figure, see www.iste.co.uk/duong/SEO1.zip*

Following this cleaning step by removing the URLs redirected to the site, the site almost complies with crawl and search engine indexing rules in terms of URL structures, rescodes, etc.

However, there is often still a detail to be corrected for pages with a canonical tag that points to other pages, not to themselves. If we find this case in a site, pages with a canonical tag that points to another page are also not indexed in search engines.

In the next section, we will explain the canonical tags and how to create a canonical plan (in-house methodology) in order to clean up the site in depth.

3.15. Canonical plan

What is a canonical tag? Before discussing the canonical plan, it is necessary to define the canonical. This tag was created in 2009 by Google, Bing and Yahoo!.

It was then used by other search engines, such as Yandex, Naver and Baidu (more recently for the Chinese search engine, with the 2016 MIP project, because Baidu had not yet taken into account canonical tags).

The canonical has a clear meaning: it prevents duplicate (or similar) content and indicates to search engines that there is a main alternative version of the page, and that its indexing should therefore be taken into account as a priority. The page containing a canonical tag, which points to another page considered as the main, is therefore less likely to be indexed by search engines.

When a webmaster or developer does not know the importance of the different pages, we recommend not setting up canonical tags. Thus, all pages can be indexed, moved up and ranked in the search results of the engines.

Nevertheless, to detect if a site has pages containing canonical tags, we use different crawl tools.

For example, by using a crawl tool, we can move up all non-indexed pages with a canonical tag and create a canonical page plan, as shown in Figure 3.32.

If the pages really are variations, i.e. pages with few elements that change in content, but have a purpose on the site, we recommend leaving the pages as they are, with the canonical pointing to the main pages.

	A	B	C
1	**Introduction :** Ce document présente les URLs dupliquées contenant une balise canonical qui pointe vers une autre page considérée comme "Master". Dans le cas de [...] ce sont des pages paginées. Les canonical permettent de limiter le Duplicate Content, mais ce n'est pas la meilleure pratique pour gérer une pagination. Il vaut mieux préférer l'utilisation des balises link rel prev next pour la pagination. Voici des recommandations pour gérer la pagination : https://docs.google.com Il faut les URLs de la colonne A doivent être redirigées en 301 vers celles de la colonne C (sans les paramètres de pagination, mais l'URL master), et ensuite faire à nouveau un plan de démaillage.		
2	Full URL	Non-Compliance Reason is Non-Self Canonical Tag	Canonical To Full URL
3	https://www..../s/F6310_coteaux-nantais?idf=6310&page=2	VRAI	https://www..../s/F6310_coteaux-nantais?page=2
4	https://www..../s/F6353_vitamont?idf=6353&page=2	VRAI	https://www..../s/F6353_vitamont?page=2
5	https://www..../s/29603_fruits-frais?idcat=29603&page=1	VRAI	https://www..../s/29603_fruits-frais?page=1
6	https://www..../s/29646_conserves-de-legumes?idcat=29646&page=1	VRAI	https://www..../s/29646_conserves-de-legumes?page=1
7	https://www..../s/29591_les-boissons-vegetales?idcat=29591&page=1	VRAI	https://www..../s/29591_les-boissons-vegetales?page=1
8	https://www..../s/29640_potages-et-soupes?idcat=29640&page=1	VRAI	https://www..../s/29640_potages-et-soupes?page=1
9	https://www..../s/29667_biscottes-brioches?idcat=29667&page=1	VRAI	https://www..../s/29667_biscottes-brioches?page=1
10	https://www..../s/F6248_celnat?idf=6248&page=1	VRAI	https://www..../s/F6248_celnat?page=1
11	https://www..../s/29660_the-et-infusion?idcat=29660&page=1	VRAI	https://www..../s/29660_the-et-infusion?page=1
12	https://www..../s/F6247_markal?idf=6247&page=2	VRAI	https://www..../s/F6247_markal?page=2
13	https://www..../s/29565_produits-bebe?idcat=29565&page=1	VRAI	https://www..../s/29565_produits-bebe?page=1

Figure 3.32. *Plan of canonical pages to be cleaned*

For all URL and pagination parameters, it is better to manage these problems in Google Search Console or in other webmaster tools of search engines (see Figure 3.33).

Figure 3.33. *Management of URL parameters that can generate duplicated content and less strategic pages*

In order to optimize the URL settings in Google Search Console, each time we click on "Change/Reset", we receive the message as shown in Figure 3.34.

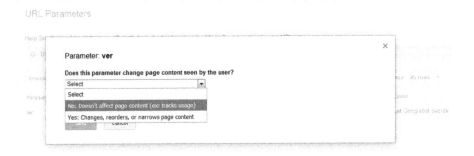

Figure 3.34. *Managing URL settings of a site as a question*

If we answer "no" to the question "do the generated parameters affect the content of the site?", this means that the page with the parameter is content duplicated on a URL that is different from the static URL (i.e. without the parameter). So GoogleBot will crawl less URLs in this typology.

If we answer "yes", it means that the page with the parameter changes the contents of the page once it is generated, and so GoogleBot will crawl this type of URL in order to also list them in its index.

Following this phase of cleaning the canonical tags (pointing an important page to itself if it is necessary to set up canonicals) and managing the URL parameters, we generally consider that the site is 85 or 90% cleaned up in terms of technical SEO. However, in some cases, it is necessary to set up log audits on the site in order to assess the site's performance and understand why some search engines do not visit certain pages.

We will address this point in the next section with the help of an external tool called OnCrawl ELK.

3.16. Log audit

The log audit methodology considered below is a methodology specific to its author, Véronique Duong. But each referrer can develop their own solution.

Log analysis, which we prefer to call "log audit", is an action for experts in the technical SEO phase.

After having carried out a "classic" technical SEO audit of the site, and before, during or after the optimization recommendations have been implemented, we can add an additional phase, which is the log audit.

In concrete terms, we will retrieve the daily logs of a site and analyze them with a log tool such as Screaming Frog Log Analyzer (the data are raw and we must generate graphs manually in order to represent the information) or OnCrawl (in this case, we do not have to create the graphs ourselves).

Figure 3.35 shows an example of graphs and data that we can produce (manually) using Screaming Frog Log Analyzer.

As we said earlier, with OnCrawl, we do not need to create graphs, because the interface generates them for us and we just have to interpret the results.

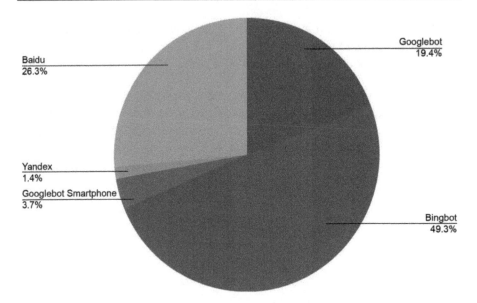

Figure 3.35. *Percentage of hits (visits) per engine. For a color version of this figure, see www.iste.co.uk/duong/SEO1.zip*

In the OnCrawl graph of Figure 3.36, we see that Googlebot crawls more and more pages of the site we manage after optimization.

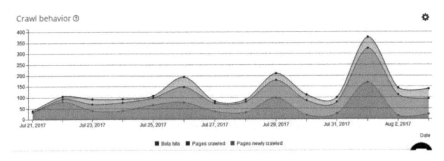

Figure 3.36. *Hits (visits) and GoogleBot behavior for an optimized site. For a color version of this figure, see www.iste.co.uk/duong/SEO1.zip*

OnCrawl's Logs Explorer provides a lot of information: the pages visited, the active or inactive pages (this means that the page has received less than one SEO visit per month), the organic visits on the page in question, etc.

FULL URL		BOTS HITS	SEO VISITS	IS NEWLY CRAWLED	IS NEWLY ACTIVE	
		16	11	true	true	
		5	0	true	false	
		5	0	true	false	
		1	0	true	false	
		1	0	true	false	
		3	0	true	false	
		1	0	true	false	

Figure 3.37. *OnCrawl Logs Explorer*

We also tested OnCrawl's open source log analyzer, and here are the steps to implement it. In terms of prerequisites, the handling of command lines, shell functions, is necessary. In addition, there is an online installation guide for OnCrawl's[7] log analyzer. Here, we followed the steps to set up the log analyzer:

– download of Docker Toolbox;

– installation of the virtual machine (VM) with which it is delivered;

– launch of the Docker terminal to operate the *docker-compose -f docker-compose.yml up –d* command.

Figure 3.38. *VM terminal with the launch of the Docker command-line-kitematic, where containers are clearly present*

---

7 "Guide d'installation de l'analyseur de Logs d'OnCrawl" (translation: OnCrawl Log Analyzer Installation Guide) available at: https://fr.oncrawl.com/seo-technique/comment-faire-de-analyse-de-fichiers-de-logs-gratuitement/.

Figure 3.39. *OnCrawl Container Logs*

Then, we placed the logs in the /logs/apache directory, then a URL was generated with the IP, and we get our graphs (see Figure 3.40).

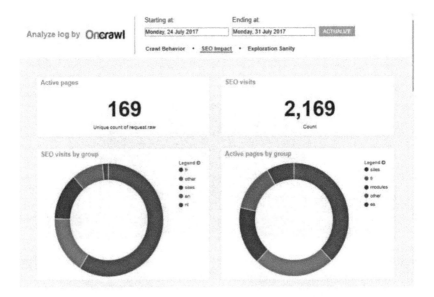

Figure 3.40. *Graphs generated by log data. For a color version of this figure, see www.iste.co.uk/duong/SEO1.zip*

There is a non-open-source version of OnCrawl's log analyzer. However, this open-source version already gives a very interesting overview of crawl page volumes and hits over customizable periods, but it is true that it does not allow in-depth analysis. For example, the tool shows us 404 pages, but we cannot see which ones by clicking on the part of the corresponding pie chart, whereas this is possible in the non-open-source version. Figure 3.41 presents an overview of the data we can get from the logs. We also have information on the active pages, and how the engines visit them and crawl them (see Figure 3.42).

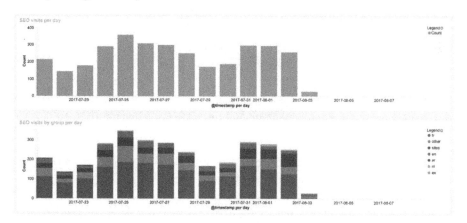

Figure 3.41. *SEO visits per day and per category per day. For a color version of this figure, see www.iste.co.uk/duong/SEO1.zip*

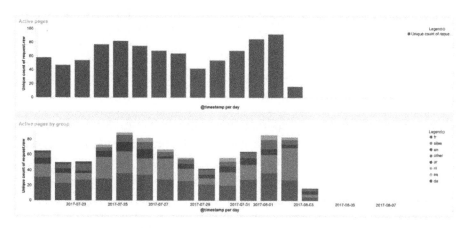

Figure 3.42. *Active pages only and by category. For a color version of this figure, see www.iste.co.uk/duong/SEO1.zip*

We can also obtain general information on the distribution of pages by rescode (see Figure 3.43).

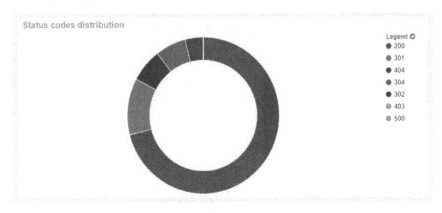

Status codes distribution

Legend ○
● 200
● 301
● 404
● 304
● 302
● 403
● 500

Figure 3.43. *Distribution of pages by rescode (analysis based on logs). For a color version of this figure, see www.iste.co.uk/duong/SEO1.zip*

Log auditing is a complementary step but may be essential for e-commerce sites with thousands of web pages. Log analysis makes it possible to better understand what is happening on a site and how search engines behave. Indirectly, a log audit makes it possible to strengthen the optimization of a site's pages and thus to better position them in search engines.

Each site is unique and we have tried, with the above points, to generalize the methods of technical SEO optimization through the cases we have studied and analyzed.

In the following sections, we remain in the technical part and they concern the tagging of HTML pages.

Indeed, in SEO, it is important for the tagging to be complete, in particular so that the semantic optimization part (see Chapter 4) is feasible in the best possible conditions.

3.17. Meta tags

In SEO, the most well-known strategic elements to optimize are certainly meta tags (or metadata).

The meta tags are composed of the tag <title> and the tag <meta name="description">, as well as the tag <meta name="keywords">, which would still be effective with an impact on semantic SEO for most Asian engines (Baidu, Naver, Sogou, Qihoo 360, etc.).

These tags must be coded in the <head></head part of a web page and must be as close as possible to the opening <head> tag (see Figure 3.44).

```
<!DOCTYPE html>
<html lang="fr">
    <head>
        <title>Consultante SEO Baidu Google certifiée - AUTOVEILLE</title>
        <meta name="description" content="AUTOVEILLE est un site de la consultante SEO certifiée CESEO, Véronique Duong,
        <meta charset="windows-1252">
        <meta name="google-site-verification" content="ct4Qqxpyqd_Rtft5rA5M1KuEFw9ieBzfhm7KXqEc5zA">
        <meta name="msvalidate.01" content="4D6170634E029BA8AB3D352E715C0BCA" />
        <meta name="baidu-site-verification" content="hSWA3QMQOE" />
        <meta name="shenma-site-verification" content="6236ff1f0391176c291dd61e920cae15_1506020733"/>
        <meta name="360-site-verification" content="39c911d75e7191d6e4402bc9a62137fe" />
        <meta name="sogou_site_verification" content="TqM4E4fgmg"/>
        <meta name='yandex-verification' content='73b627366e567f82' />
        <meta name="naver-site-verification" content="2c8af0132bf7fbadb3780ccb4e3cd5fa31d70b02"/>
        <meta name="viewport" content="initial-scale=1.0,width=device-width"/>
```

Figure 3.44. *Tagging of meta tags, including the title and meta description at the very beginning of the web page. For a color version of this figure, see www.iste.co.uk/duong/SEO1.zip*

The other tags we show in Figure 3.44 are also called meta tags and metadata.

Meta tags are not mandatory tags to be implemented in a website. There are websites with only the tags <head>, <title>, <link rel CSS>, etc., without the tags <meta>; but this type of site is not SEO friendly and has more difficulty in finding its way up correctly in search engine results.

In most CMS, such as WordPress, Prestashop, Drupal, Magento, etc., there are specific fields or modules, such as Yoast[8], to implement meta tags.

Figure 3.45 illustrates the example of Yoast.

After implementing the meta tags, we recommend setting up the <HN> tags, also called heading tags or heading titles. Indeed, after the meta tags, search engines browse these titles, which constitute the semantic structure of the page.

---

8 "Yoast Module for SEO on WordPress", available at: https://yoast.com/.

Figure 3.45. *Interface for editing the meta tags title and meta description in Yoast (in French)*

3.18. Heading tags

After meta tags, search engines will scan the heading titles of a web page. These titles are placed in the <body> tag of the site and must follow this hierarchy (from 1 to 6) in order to be technically optimized:

– H1: level 1 title containing the subject or main information. This tag has the most semantic influence compared to the other five;

– H2: level 2 title containing a subtitle of H1. This tag remains important for SEO, but has a slightly lower influence than H1;

– H3: level 3 title containing a subtitle of H2. This tag is specific to the page and generally gives more precise information than H1 and H2, but it has less semantic influence than H1 and H2;

– H4: level 4 title containing small titles for each paragraph. This tag is in the detail of the points covered per page. Its impact in SEO is minimal. However, it must still contain keywords;

– H5: level 5 title containing specific product or element names. This tag has almost no impact in terms of semantic SEO influence, but it allows the information to be structured well, so you must also put keywords in it;

– H6: level 6 title (the last one) containing very specific elements about a product, concept or idea. This tag is rarely used, as most sites do not go into this depth of information.

Figure 3.46 provides an example of well-organized heading titles.

https://www.seo-camp.org/

⊟ 19 headings

‹h1› SEO CAMP

    ‹h2› L'association du référencement

    ‹h2› Événements SEO CAMP

        ‹h3› SEO CAMPUS PARIS 2018

Figure 3.46. *HN tag hierarchy (from general to specific) (in French)*

HN tags must contain keywords, as they have an impact on SEO in terms of keywords, content and editorial. Avoid using HN tags to create call-to-action buttons or put non-strategic information in them without keywords.

For example, in the case of Figure 3.47, HN tags are not optimized for SEO.

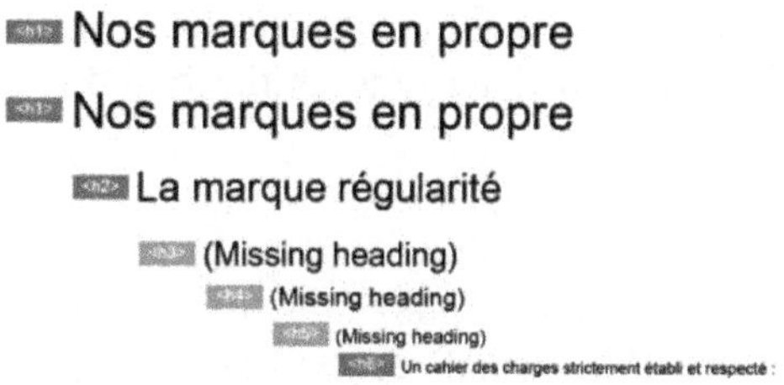

‹h1› Nos marques en propre

‹h1› Nos marques en propre

   ‹h2› La marque régularité

     ‹h3› (Missing heading)

      ‹h4› (Missing heading)

       ‹h5› (Missing heading)

        ‹h6› Un cahier des charges strictement établi et respecté :

Figure 3.47. *Lack of keywords and content in the heading titles of the page (in French)*

If, by reading the heading titles alone, an Internet user or a search engine cannot understand the main information on the page and there are no keywords present in these titles, we consider it necessary to rewrite and optimize them.

Heading titles have no character limit but should be between 5 and 10 words maximum.

Following the implementation of heading titles tags, we are interested in linguistic tags called hreflang.

3.19. Hreflang tagging

Hreflang attributes are linguistic tags created by Google to manage multilingual sites that are on the same domain. Typically, international sites present such problems. In order to show the right language version to search engines, it is absolutely necessary to tag multilingual web pages correctly otherwise the implementation may not work.

At the time of writing (end of 2018), hreflang tags only worked with Google, Yandex and Seznam (Czech Republic engine) but did not work with Baidu, Qihoo 360, Shenma, Sogou, Naver and Yahoo! Japan (almost all Asian search engines).

If an owner has a site with several language versions, it is necessary to put the tag *<link rel="alternate" href="example.com/language-folder/" hreflang="language-country"/>* in the *<head>* part of the multilingual web pages.

In addition, it is also possible to implement the tag <link rel="alternate" href="http://example.com/" hreflang="x-default"/> to define a default language, which Google will determine as the best for the user if no page seems to be qualified for the user.

There is a precise syntax to implement the hreflang language tags. In the methodology proposed by Google, the value of the hreflang attribute allows the language (in ISO 639-1 format) as well as the region (optional, in ISO 3166-1 Alpha 2 format) of another version of the URL to be indicated.

Here is the exact syntax:

– en: content in English, regardless of region;

– en-GB: English content for Internet users located in the United Kingdom;

– en-ES: English content for Internet users located in Spain.

We must always have a couple of "language-countries", namely "fr-CA" for French-language content intended for Internet users in Canada and "es-FR" for Spanish-language content intended for Internet users in France. It is important to respect this syntax, otherwise hreflang tags are ignored.

For Chinese languages, we have a subtlety because it must be written in the following syntax (in ISO 15924 format):

– zh-Hant: traditional Chinese;

– zh-Hans: simplified Chinese.

For example, the zh-Hans-TW code refers to Taiwanese Internet users who speak simplified Chinese.

In a study conducted by a major player in the SEO field, SEMrush[9], we found that most of the problems with hreflang tags are related to their implementation and incorrect syntax (see Figure 3.48).

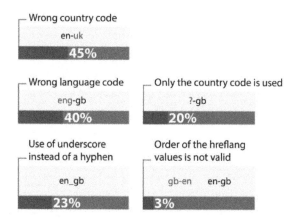

PROBLEMS WITH HREFLANG VALUES

Figure 3.48. *Errors and problems with hreflang values (SEMrush study). For a color version of this figure, see www.iste.co.uk/duong/SEO1.zip*

In Google Search Console, it is possible to track the performance of hreflang tags and see that they have not generated errors (see Figure 3.49).

---

9 "Common errors when implementing hreflang", available at: https://autoveille.info/ 2017/07/24/errors-common-during-the-inclusion-of-hreflang/attributes.

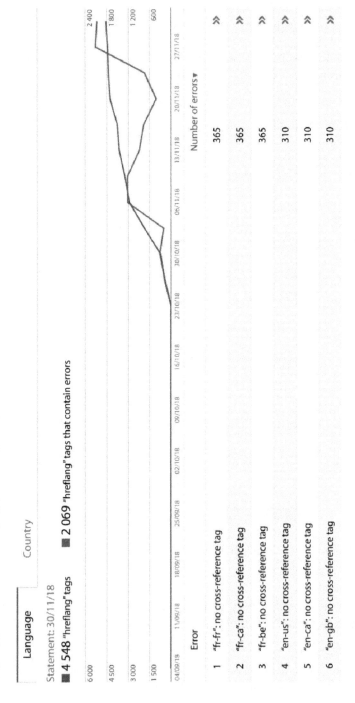

Figure 3.49. *Tracking hreflang tags in Google Search Console. For a color version of this figure, see www.iste.co.uk/duong/SEO1.zip*

Google Search Console allows you to see how hreflang tags evolve and whether some of them generate errors. Once the hreflang tags are implemented successfully and the pages are declared in the right language at the level of the tag *<html lang="language">*, (Western) search engines should be able to send the right language version to Internet users who speak the same language but are located in different parts of the world.

Following (or in parallel with) the implementation of the hreflang tags, it is also necessary to work on the implementation of alternative attributes, especially for images. In the next section, we will discuss the explanation of alt attributes and where to code them.

3.20. Alt attribute tagging

Alternative attributes are best known for images. Indeed, Google Images, as well as other image engines, read this attribute to understand the description of the image and to index the image according to the keywords that appear there.

In concrete terms, alt attributes are found in the image tags and are presented in the form as follows:

<img src="name.jpg" **alt= "Keywords - Product name / Category - Brand"**/>

It is important to implement this attribute in the HTML codes of the image tags from the beginning of the work, so that the semantic optimization of these attributes is done systematically afterwards, when the site owners must fill in the alternative description of the images.

In CMS, such as WordPress, Drupal and Magento, there are fields called "alternative text", "alt" or "descriptive text" to designate the alt attribute of images (see Figure 3.50).

Once all the alt attributes of the images are successfully implemented, we can move on to optimizing secondary markup such as rich snippets, Open Graph (Facebook) meta tags or Twitter Card meta tags.

Figure 3.50. *Management of alt attributes in a CMS such as WordPress (in French) with information included such as title, key, alternative text, description and URL*

3.21. Rich snippets tagging

Organization of Schemas

The schemas are a set of 'types', each associated with a set of properties. The types are arranged in a hierarchy. The core vocabulary currently consists of 598 Types, 862 Properties, and 114 Enumeration values.

Browse the full hierarchy:

- One page per type
- Full list of types, shown on one page

Or you can jump directly to a commonly used type:

- Creative works: CreativeWork, Book, Movie, MusicRecording, Recipe, TVSeries ...
- Embedded non-text objects: AudioObject, ImageObject, VideoObject
- Event
- Health and medical types: notes on the health and medical types under MedicalEntity.
- Organization
- Person
- Place, LocalBusiness, Restaurant ...
- Product, Offer, AggregateOffer
- Review, AggregateRating
- Action

Figure 3.51. *The most commonly used types of schemas*

Schema.org tags are metadata tags that allow you to add additional information to a web page. There are several types of schema.org tags. Figure 3.51 provides an extract from the most common schemas.

In Figure 3.53, we will detail an example of a schema for the breadcrumb trail, which turns out to be one of the schemas regularly used on sites.

On schema.org, there is a special page on breadcrumbs and this provides examples of codes to implement to generate the rich snippet in Google.

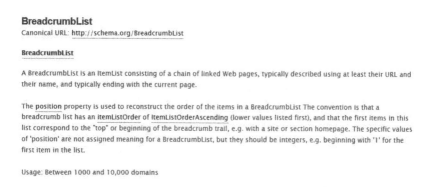

BreadcrumbList
Canonical URL: http://schema.org/BreadcrumbList

BreadcrumbList

A BreadcrumbList is an ItemList consisting of a chain of linked Web pages, typically described using at least their URL and their name, and typically ending with the current page.

The position property is used to reconstruct the order of the items in a BreadcrumbList The convention is that a breadcrumb list has an itemListOrder of ItemListOrderAscending (lower values listed first), and that the first items in this list correspond to the "top" or beginning of the breadcrumb trail, e.g. with a site or section homepage. The specific values of 'position' are not assigned meaning for a BreadcrumbList, but they should be integers, e.g. beginning with '1' for the first item in the list.

Usage: Between 1000 and 10,000 domains

Figure 3.52. *The schema.org page detailing the breadcrumb list schema*

Property	On Types	Description
breadcrumb	WebPage	A set of links that can help a user understand and navigate a website hierarchy.

Examples

Example 1

| Without Markup | Microdata | RDFa | JSON-LD |

```
<ol>
  <li>
    <a href="https://example.com/dresses">Dresses</a>
  </li>
  <li>
    <a href="https://example.com/dresses/real">Real Dresses</a>
  </li>
</ol>
```

Figure 3.53. *Simple HTML code, without schema.org markup for the breadcrumb trail*

Figure 3.53 shows the meta itemprop code to be used to generate the breadcrumb trail in rich snippets.

In the "Microdata" tab in Figure 3.53, we can access the source code that generates rich snippets with the breadcrumb trail, which will be displayed in Google's search results.

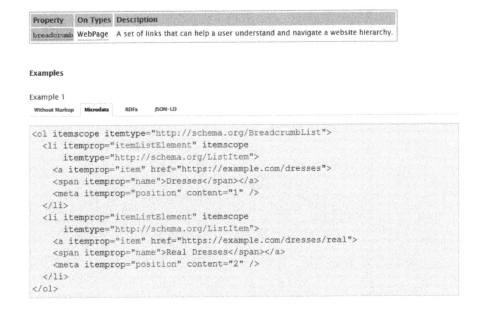

Property	On Types	Description
breadcrumb	WebPage	A set of links that can help a user understand and navigate a website hierarchy.

Examples

Example 1

| Without Markup | Microdata | RDFa | JSON-LD |

```
<ol itemscope itemtype="http://schema.org/BreadcrumbList">
  <li itemprop="itemListElement" itemscope
      itemtype="http://schema.org/ListItem">
    <a itemprop="item" href="https://example.com/dresses">
    <span itemprop="name">Dresses</span></a>
    <meta itemprop="position" content="1" />
  </li>
  <li itemprop="itemListElement" itemscope
      itemtype="http://schema.org/ListItem">
    <a itemprop="item" href="https://example.com/dresses/real">
    <span itemprop="name">Real Dresses</span></a>
    <meta itemprop="position" content="2" />
  </li>
</ol>
```

Figure 3.54. *The same HTML source code as in Figure 3.52, but tagged with schema.org's meta itemprop. For a color version of this figure, see www.iste.co.uk/duong/SEO1.zip*

In the search results, we have a breadcrumb trail that is formed within the snippet (see Figure 3.55).

Soft and Chewy Chocolate Chip Cookies Recipe - Live Well Bake Often

https://www.livewellbakeoften.com › Cookies ▼ Traduire cette page

★★★★★ Note : 5 - 46 votes - 2 h 27 min

13 juin 2018 - These chocolate chip **cookies** are extra soft, thick, and chewy. This is my FAVORITE **recipe** for chocolate chips **cookies** and they turn out perfect ...

Figure 3.55. *Breadcrumb trail apparent in the rich snippet of the optimized site*

With rich snippets, we find that the click rate on search results is 20–30% higher in comparison with traditional search results (without rich snippets).

Apart from rich snippets, there have been rich cards since 2016. Rich cards are the advanced format of rich snippets.

Like rich snippets, rich cards use schema.org's structured/micro data to display interesting content and to provide a better user experience on mobile devices.

Figure 3.56. *Classic search results versus rich snippets versus rich cards*

For site owners and webmasters, it is a strategy that helps generate interest, differentiate terms in search results and attract more Internet users to the pages. For example, if an owner has a recipe site, it is possible to generate an enhanced preview of the content with an image on the front page of each dish. This visual format helps web users find what they want right away.

For this rich card format, Google started with recipes and movies. First, rich cards appeared in mobile search results in English on google.com. Google is working on expanding this format to other versions of its engine. Google regularly updates its documentation on rich cards[10] in its online support. Following the implementation of all the techniques mentioned

10 "Documentation on Google Rich Cards", available at: https://developers.google.com/ search/docs/guides/intro-structured-data.

above, we consider that a site is 95% optimized. There are still additional details, which consist of the implementation of social network tags and social network share buttons in order to easily share a web page on Facebook, Twitter, etc.

3.22. Open Graph meta tagging

Open Graph markup was launched by Facebook in 2010 and is now owned by the Open Web Foundation. The objective was to allow easier integration between Facebook and other sites by displaying rich graph objects with the same features as Facebook objects. The idea was to have a certain degree of control over the information that was shared.

The main social network platforms now offer this tag, even if Twitter has developed its own for Twitter Cards, which we explain below (knowing that Twitter still accepts Open Graph if necessary).

The information is sent via the Open Graph meta tags in the <head> part of the code of your site.

Figure 3.57 provides an example of SEO/SMO (social media optimization) optimized Open Graph code.

```
<meta property="og:type" content="website" />
<meta property="og:title" content="# AUTOVEILLE SEO | Consulting SEO @veroduong - veronique-duong.com" />
<meta property="og:description" content="Blog SEO sur le SEO Google, SEO Baidu, SEO Bing et le Webmarketing par Véronique Duong, SEO
<meta property="og:url" content="https://autoveille.info/" />
<meta property="og:site_name" content="# AUTOVEILLE SEO | Consulting SEO @veroduong - veronique-duong.com" />
<meta property="og:image" content="https://secure.gravatar.com/blavatar/03fbce14530b633724fa087b5c70a14c?s=200&amp;ts=1543776875" />
<meta property="og:image:width" content="200" />
<meta property="og:image:height" content="200" />
<meta property="og:locale" content="fr_FR" />
```

Figure 3.57. *Example of HTML source code to generate Open Graph data*

By following the Open Graph tag syntax, it is possible to quickly set up information sharing panels in social networks, including Facebook.

Figure 3.58 shows an example of information data automatically generated using Open Graph meta tags (we have pasted the URL of the page containing the Open Graph meta tags in the Facebook social network publication field).

Figure 3.58. *Post automatically generated on Facebook using Open Graph meta tags (in French)*

Open Graph meta tags, once filled in, save real time for shared web pages because Internet users do not need to write a post. For an e-commerce site, it is interesting to set up Open Graph meta tags for the main product pages, news, etc.

In addition to Open Graph meta tags, there are Twitter Cards that have the same principle and similar objectives.

3.23. Twitter meta tagging

Twitter Cards are protocols that allow you to attach photos, videos and other interactive media to Twitter publications in order to bring traffic to a website.

Twitter provides a wide range of maps. In addition, Twitter Cards can be integrated into web pages with a few lines in HTML. Users referring to content with a tweet will have a card added to it, which will be visible to all their subscribers.

Twitter Cards are a good methodology that combines social networks and SEO in an SEO strategy, because they improve engagement and increase click rate and conversions.

Twitter Cards can therefore accelerate the reach of content on social networks and develop SEO.

There are five different types of Twitter Cards:

– Summary Card;

– Summary Card with large image;

– Player Card;

– App Card;

– Lead Generation Card.

Example of Summary Card tagging is as follows:

```
<meta name="twitter :card" content="summary"/>
<meta name="twitter :site" content="@yoursite"/>
<meta name="twitter :title" content="Your Title"/>
<meta name="twitter :description" content="Your description."/>
<meta name="twitter :image" content="https://where-your-image-is-
hosted/name.jpg"/>
```

Example of Summary Card tagging with large image is as follows:

```
<meta name="twitter :card" content="summary_large_image">
<meta name="twitter :site" content="@yourwebsite">
<meta name="twitter :creator" content="@yourtwitterhandle">
<meta name="twitter :title" content="your title">
<meta name="twitter :description" content="your description.">
<meta name="twitter :image" content="https://where-your-image-is-
hosted/name.jpg">
```

Figure 3.59 illustrates the example of the Summary Card with large image.

TechCrunch ✓
@TechCrunch

☑ Follow

Everything you need to know about the Amazon Fire Phone
trib.al/WcAExlJ
4:40 PM - 23 Jul 2014

TechCrunch

Hands On With The Amazon Fire Phone I TechCrunch
Announced last month, the Amazon Fire Phone is the company's first
attempt at mobile hardware. Like its cousins in the Kindle Fire line of
tablets, it runs a fork of Android and gives you...

View on web

↩   ⟲ 80   ♥ 44

Figure 3.59. *Example of Twitter's Summary Card with large image*

Example of App Card tagging is as follows:"

```
<meta name="twitter :card" content="app">
<meta name="twitter :site" content="@yourwebsite">
<meta name="twitter :description" content="your description">
<meta name="twitter :app :country" content="your country like US">
<meta name="twitter :app :name :iphone" content="your iphone app name">
<meta name="twitter :app :id :iphone" content="your iphone app ID">
<meta name="twitter :app :url :iphone" content="your iphone app URL">
<meta name="twitter :app :name :ipad" content="your ipad app name">
<meta name="twitter :app :id :ipad" content="your ipad app ID">
<meta name="twitter :app :url :ipad" content="your ipad app URL">
<meta name="twitter :app :name :googleplay" content="your googleplay app
name">
<meta name="twitter :app :id :googleplay" content="your googleplay add
ID"
```

Twitter Cards generate automatically optimized and relevant publications. Setting them up allows the site to generate more traffic via SEO and SMO channels.

In the next step, we recommend setting up share buttons on strategic web pages of a site, so that Internet users can easily share them on social networks.

3.24. Social network share buttons

After implementing all the actions and elements mentioned above, it is interesting to set up social network share buttons to allow Internet users to share product and article pages on social networks more efficiently and quickly.

In the West, there are modules like AddThis, which allow the majority of social network share buttons to be implemented (see Figure 3.60).

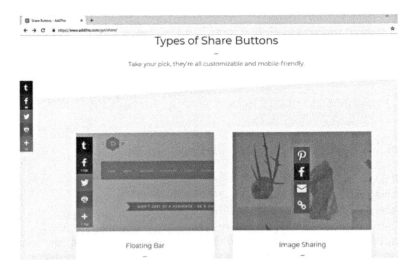

Figure 3.60. *Several types of share buttons proposed by AddThis*

In China, there are equivalents of AddThis such as JiaThis and bShare, allowing share buttons for major Chinese social networks such as Weibo, QQ and Renren to be generated (see Figure 3.61).

Figure 3.61. *Buttons to share Chinese social networks via bShare*

The JiaThis platform offers several formats of share buttons (see Figure 3.62).

Figure 3.62. *Chinese social networking share button platform, JiaThis*

We regularly use JiaThis for our projects, because it offers a wide range of possibilities to customize share buttons. Alternatively, it is possible to directly implement the JavaScript codes offered by the various social networks to share pages. For example, the Twitter share button can be set up with the code shown in Figure 3.63.

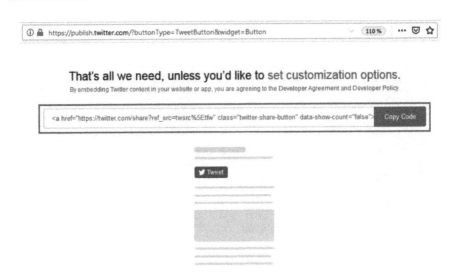

Figure 3.63. *Code to generate the Twitter share button (customizable)*

After implementing the social network share buttons, we consider that the website pages are technically optimized at 98%, with URLs worked, cleaned, optimized, etc. There is still 2% more work to do, because it is still possible to further optimize a website's source code with lighter JavaScript, CSS, HTML code, etc.

3.25. Page lifecycle management (articles and products)

In a site, there are pages that are deactivated because the products or news no longer exist, or because there are new pages coming in: this is part of the life of the site. However, as we have seen in the previous sections, for a site to respond perfectly to search engine compliance, it must only offer pages that are in HTML, in rescode 200, and that do not have canonical tags pointing to another page.

We therefore propose two solutions to manage the lifecycle of pages that no longer exist. And we recommend taking the first solution:

1) leave the product or article pages that no longer have stock or are no longer up to date in 200 (they should not be disabled in order to avoid a 404 error);

2) redirect the product pages without stock to the parent category page (in 301).

If the first solution is chosen, it is necessary to have relevant content on the pages and to have an insert with similar products to offer, so that Internet users can choose a product or article similar to what they wanted to find in the first place.

If the second solution is chosen, it should be noted that each redirection adds 300–500 msec for loading a page. It is therefore important to optimize the time it takes to display pages on mobile phones and PCs.

An important point, which we would like to remind the reader of, is that it is essential to avoid cascading redirections (i.e. from page A to page B, then from page B to page C).

In section 3.26, we will discuss the subject of page seasonality (holidays, sales, promotions, etc.).

3.26. Seasonality of pages

Depending on the periods and seasons each year, the site undergoes several changes: new collections, sales, special pages for holidays, etc. To meet the demand while remaining well optimized for SEO, we also suggest two solutions:

1) disentangle (remove from the internal linking) the seasonal pages after the period concerned, by changing titles and meta-descriptions, so that they appear less in the search results of the engines;

2) remove the products when the event has passed, but leave the network page on the site (changing category if necessary).

In this case, we recommend the first solution, because it truly allows you to remove the pages corresponding to the holidays when they are over. As soon as the periods concerned return, it is simply a case of rewriting them in the structure of the site so that they appear in the search results. The pages must remain in rescode 200 and offer content, even if they are no longer in the website's internal linking.

For example, the company shown in Figure 3.64 leaves the product pages without stock online (in rescode 200), specifying in the content that it does not know when the product will be restocked.

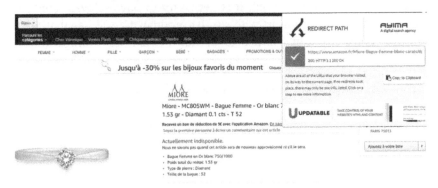

Figure 3.64. *Example of management of out of stock pages, rescode 200, but content indicating product unavailability*

Ideally, all e-commerce sites should manage their product pages using this method. Thus, in terms of SEO, these sites offer pages in 200 with interesting content and similar products that can be discovered when browsing the site.

When we talk about page management, pagination is also a very important detail to consider in SEO, so as not to create duplicate content.

3.27. Pagination of pages on a site

On most sites, it is essential to have pagination between the site pages. To manage the previous and following pages, there are solutions to avoid creating duplicate content with a high similarity rate between page 1 and page 2, and so on. Here, we provide tips for managing web page pagination:

– by default, search engines should not be allowed to index paginated web pages;

– paginated pages should only be indexed if the content is dense (more than 1,000 words per page);

– it is always necessary to add a canonical tag on page 1 of all paginated pages;

– it is always necessary to add a nofollow attribute on all links placed on paginated pages;

– you must configure the URL settings in the Search Console;

– it is necessary to configure the URLs for the paginated pages in order to easily add a rule in the robots.txt, so as not to index them;

– it is necessary to add a meta noindex and nofollow tag in the meta-robots;

– you should never add the URLs of the paginated content to the sitemap.xml;

– do not show the links on pages 2, 3, 4, 5, [...], 10, 11, 12, etc., at the end of the content, but only a following link (link rel next) and a previous link (link rel prev) in order to not dilute the authority of the page;

– use links or headers rel="next" and rel="prev" to indicate the relationship between the different site URLs.

It is possible to use HTML links or HTTP headers to indicate the next or previous segment of an article spread over several pages.

Here is the syntax for http headers:

– link: <www.example.com/cats_part_3; rel="next"> for the next segment of the article;

– link: <www.example.com/cats_part_1; rel="prev"> for the previous segment of the article.

For tags <link> HTML (recommended in our case, for SEO), it is necessary to place appropriate <link> tags in the <head> element of the page:

– <link rel="next" href="next_page_URL"> for the next segment of the article;

– <link rel="prev" href="previous_page_url"> for the previous segment of the article.

Figure 3.65 provides an example in tabular form.

Example

Here is an example of an article on three pages which uses HTML links in terms of its `<head>` tagging.

cats_part_1	cats_part_2	cats_part_3
`<link rel="next" href="cats_part_2>`	`<link rel="next" href="cats_part_3>` `<link rel="prev" href="cats_part_1>`	`<link rel="prev" href="cats_part_2>`

Figure 3.65. *Management of pagination with rel=next and rel=prev links*

Once pagination is optimized, internal duplicate content cases are reduced and search engines should only find relevant and strategic URLs to index. In this way, the site's crawl budget will not be disrupted either. In this chapter, we have covered all the main points to crawl, index and position a site in search engines. In Chapter 4, we will discuss the points related to semantic and editorial optimization, i.e. web writing in SEO.

Semantic SEO, Editorial and Copywriting

4.1. Optimization of the *title* tag

The <title> tag is the tag that would have the most influence in terms of impact on SEO. This is the title of the search result extract that you see in search engines.

For all search engines (Google, Baidu, Yandex, Naver, Yahoo! Japan, etc.), this tag is strategic, because it must provide the answer to the search or the request that an Internet user makes in the search bar.

In HTML code, the <title> tag is presented in the form detailed in Figure 4.1.

```
<!DOCTYPE html>
<html lang="fr">
    <head>
        <title>Consultante SEO Baidu Google certifiée - AUTOVEILLE</title>
        <meta name="description" content="AUTOVEILLE est un site de la consultante SEO certifiée CESEO, Véronique Duong,
```

Figure 4.1. *HTML <title> tag. For a color version of this figure, see www.iste.co.uk/duong/SEO1.zip*

The title is the place where we must put relevant information in response to Internet users' search requests. It is also in this area that we must insert one or two strategic keywords. Keywords are often those that are selected when analyzing keywords.

It is also possible to connect directly to online tools such as Google Keyword Planner or Google Trends[1] to see if the selected keywords are searched or popular (monthly search volume) and deserve to be placed in the <title> tags of web pages.

Figure 4.2 provides an overview of the <title> tag displayed in Google.

| AUTOVEILLE: Consultante SEO Baidu Google certifiée |

autoveille.free.fr/ ▾

AUTOVEILLE est un site de la consultante SEO certifiée CESEO, Véronique Duong, passionnée par le SEO Google et Baidu. Veille SEO et astuces SEO ...

Figure 4.2. *The title displayed in Google*

It is possible for Google to rewrite the <title> tags regarding the user's request. In the example in Figure 4.2, we see that in the HTML code the word order of the <title> tag is not the same as in the display of the title in the search result.

For other search engines, we did not find any automatic rewriting of titles during our experiments and tests.

The title also has a character limit and this limit varies according to the engine. Here are the official data we have for each known engine:

– Google: about 50 characters (including spaces) for the title;

– Baidu: about 20 Chinese characters (including spaces) for the title;

– Naver: about 15 Korean characters (including spaces) for the title;

– Yandex: about 60 characters (including spaces) for the title;

– Yahoo! Japan: between 15 and 20 Japanese characters for the title.

Here are the title formats that we recommend by page typology:

– home page: Brand | Keyword | Category or product names;

– categories page: Category name | Keyword | Brand;

– product page: Product name | Keyword | Brand;

– written article pages: Title of the article | Keyword (if any) | Brand.

1 "Google Trends", available at: https://trends.google.com/trends/?geo=US.

The other pages (such as legal notice pages, my account, my cart, etc.), which are less relevant or important, can be automatically optimized by a variable that will systematically fill their titles.

Once the <title> tags are optimized, we can start optimizing the <meta name="description"> tags.

4.2. Optimization of the meta description tag

The tag <meta name="description" content="..."> is the tag that allows us to add a description of a sentence in the attribute "content" in order to introduce the elements that Internet users can read in the web page.

Ideally, this tag should be placed just after the <title> tag in the HTML source code.

The meta description is displayed below the title in search engine results (see Figure 4.3).

Consultant SEO | SEO Digital Evangelist | Véronique Duong
autoveille.free.fr/veronique.html ▼

Véronique Duong est ingénieure linguiste et SEO certifiée CESEO. SEO Digital Evangelist sur Google, Baidu, etc. à Paris ! Pour en savoir plus, cliquez !

Figure 4.3. *The meta description displayed in Google*

For Google, meta description has no direct impact on the ranking of web pages in its search results. This description is more intended to encourage Internet users to click on the results.

As a result, you have to put in calls to action, interesting marketing messages, baselines that capture the attention of users. Keywords must also be added to meta descriptions, so that they respond to users' requests from the first lines of reading in meta tags (title and meta description).

Meta descriptions also have a character limit to respect. Here are the limits according to the search engines:

– Google: about 156 characters, including spaces;

– Baidu: between 80 and 100 Chinese characters, including spaces;

– Naver: between 40 and 45 Korean characters, including spaces;

– Yandex: between 155 and 160 Russian characters, including spaces;

– Yahoo! Japan: between 45 and 50 Japanese characters, including spaces.

By page typology, we can also recommend possible meta description formats. For example:

– home page: *discover the world of BRAND, specialist in KEYWORD 1, KEYWORD 2. Visit our official website EXAMPLE.COM*;

– categories page: *discover our ranges of CATEGORY NAMES or COLLECTIONS. Visit our official website to learn more about the BRAND, specialist in KEYWORD 1, KEYWORD 2* (possibly);

– product page: *discover our product PRODUCT NAME, specializing in KEYWORD 1, KEYWORD 2. Visit our official website EXAMPLE.COM*;

– articles page: *discover our new article: TITLE OF THE ARTICLE. Visit our official website EXAMPLE.COM.*

For other less strategic and relevant pages, it is possible to fill in the meta-descriptions with a generic sentence that only explains what these pages offer in terms of content (legal notices, user's personal account, shopping cart, etc.).

Following the optimization of meta-descriptions, we can optimize the heading titles tags that are H1, H2, H3, etc.

4.3. Optimization of heading titles (H1, H2, H3)

Heading titles tags are editorial titles that structure information within a web page. As we have already mentioned in Chapter 3 on technical SEO, after meta tags, search engines scan the page and read the tags <body>, <h1>, <h2>, <h3>, etc.

The <hn> tags have a certain influence in terms of semantic SEO, because they often contain the most important data and structure the importance of information in the content.

Within these tags, we must find popular and searched keywords. These tags should not contain elements such as "click here" and "learn more", because this type of content does not have strategic keywords and should not be placed in strategic tags such as heading titles.

Unlike meta tags (titles and meta-descriptions), heading titles tags have no character limits, but this does not mean that we can put a lot of information in these tags. A maximum of ten words per <hn> tag is sufficient to place keywords and relevant information.

Figure 4.4 shows an example of optimized <hn> tags.

http://autoveille.free.fr/recherche-developpement-intelligence-artificielle.html

⊟6 headings

<h1> AUTOVEILLE R&D en automatisation de crawler web et veille stratégique

<h2> Les recherches et les études pour une veille automatisée

<h3> Automatisation des étapes chronophages en SEO grâce au TAL

<h3> Pour information uniquement : Automatiser la veille grâce aux compétences de l'ingénierie linguistique

<h4> Les outils de la chaîne de traitements pour constituer un référentiel
<h4> Les fonctionnements des outils de corpus Perl

Figure 4.4. *Filled and optimized editorial titles*

The editorial titles in Figure 4.4 are written and optimized in a structured way to bring information from the most general to the most specific. The web page in Figure 4.4 focuses on web crawler research and development and business intelligence.

H1 contains very generic information, and the further we go in the order of heading titles, the more specific information we have. We note that at the H4 level, we find a specific subject with the "functioning of Perl corpus tools", which speaks of a specific computer language (Perl here) and the mechanisms of the tools.

The idea of heading titles is to prioritize information in this way. This is our methodology, which works to optimize the content of a web page and to create a kind of detailed plan within the page. Once the editorial titles are well implemented, content writing is also more fluid and quicker to implement.

Before moving on to the content writing phase, it is also necessary to optimize the URLs (links) of the site. If URLs are poorly written, this will affect their readability and navigation.

4.4. Optimization of URLs (URL rewriting)

URL optimization has a very specific name in SEO: it is called "URL rewriting". The idea is to rewrite the URLs of a site, so that they are easier to read, contain keywords and are easy to remember. Often, with URL settings related to faceted navigation, filter selection and category selection in e-commerce sites, URLs are presented in the following form:

https://www.example.com/search?category=dress&brand=name&color=red&size=38

This type of URL is not SEO friendly and can cause content duplication problems. The main URLs are those that do not contain any parameters. All those that contain them are often variations of the main URLs.

We discussed this in Chapter 3 (in the section devoted to the canonical plan) and it should be recalled here that duplicated content, even poorly managed, can be penalized by the site, because it sends a bad signal to search engines.

To manage URL settings, as we also mentioned earlier, it is possible to do this with Google's Search Console (for example) in "URL Settings" (see Chapter 3, section 3.18).

In this section, the idea is to rewrite poorly written URLs, such as:

https://www.example.com/search?category=dress&brand=name&color=red&size=38

And to transform them into a shorter and more readable type of URL, such as:

https://www.example.com/dress/brand/red/38/

The idea is to have URLs that are readable by Internet users and search engines. Cleaner URLs are also indexed more quickly in engines. To manage

URL rewriting, you must go to the site's .htaccess file and make the changes inside.

However, there are some technical precautions to take into account before rewriting URLs: if a site is hosted on a shared server, it is not guaranteed that the host has enabled URL rewriting support, mainly for security reasons. Likewise, if a site is provided on a free hosting provider (such as wordpress. com), it is unlikely that URL rewriting is possible. We recommend investing in paid hosting (with a domain name), because there are more advantages for making good SEO.

URLs must not contain accented characters (à, é, è, ù, ô, etc.) or special characters (¢, ß, ¥, £, ™, ©, ®, ª, ×, ÷, ±, ², etc.) because they will be incorrectly encoded (bytes will be present instead) and they can generate errors.

Therefore, HTML file names should be named correctly from the beginning, with keywords and hyphens as a separator. Underscores "_" are not considered as separators. Underscores should therefore be avoided.

A good URL must have the following format:

example.com/category/sub-section/product(.html)

It is not mandatory to have the extension .html in the HTML file names and this has no impact on the page's SEO.

If we use a content management system (CMS), it is the slugs or URIs that must be optimized. Figure 4.5 shows an example of a slug in WordPress.

Figure 4.5. *URI or permalink (green box) to be optimized in WordPress. For a color version of this figure, see www.iste.co.uk/duong/SEO1.zip*

When we rewrite URLs, we perform a 301 redirection (recommended). Figure 4.6 shows how this works in the rules of the .ht access file.

```
#----------------------------------------------------
# Répertoire : /articles/
#----------------------------------------------------

# Le serveur doit suivre les liens symboliques :
Options +FollowSymlinks

# Activation du module de réécriture d'URL :
RewriteEngine on

#----------------------------------------------------
# Règles de réécriture d'URL :
#----------------------------------------------------

# Article sans numéro de page :
RewriteRule ^article-([0-9]+)-([0-9]+).html$   /articles/article.php?id=$1&rub
rique=$2 [L]

# Article avec numéro de page :
RewriteRule ^article-([0-9]+)-([0-9]+)-([0-9]+).html   /articles/article.php?i
d=$1&page=$2&rubrique=$3 [L]
```

Figure 4.6. *URL rewriting rules in the .htaccess (source: WebRankInfo[2])*

An important point to note is that there must be no carriage return on a rewrite rule line. Lines beginning with the hash sign (#) are comments. These lines are totally ignored by the URL rewriting module. Each .htaccess file is specific to a directory; we have made it a habit to indicate at the top of this file the location of the directory on the site. Each directory of the site will therefore have to propose its own .htaccess file. The .htaccess file can consist of a series of rewriting rules. Each rule is written on a single line and respects the following format:

RewriteRule URL_A_REECRIRE URL_REECRITE

The RewriteRule is a directive specific to the *mod_rewrite* module indicating that the line defines a rewrite rule. Then we have the directive for the URL to be rewritten, i.e. the "clean" URL without physical existence on the server. Finally, the rewritten URL comes, i.e. the URL as it will be called internally on the server. These three elements must be written on a single line and separated by one or more spaces each time.

Normally, as an SEO specialist, this technical part of URL rewriting must be done by the site developer, not the SEO consultant themself. This is part of the phases and milestones in SEO project management presented in Chapter 2. The element that the SEO specialist must provide here is a URL

---

2 "WebRankInfo", available at: https://www.webrankinfo.com.

rewriting plan with all the old URLs that are present, rewritten into new URLs. The deliverable can be presented in an Excel type spreadsheet.

Following the rewriting of URLs, making them more readable and their optimization more effective with keywords, we can start optimizing the textual content of the site.

4.5. Optimization of text content

In this section, we will discuss the main concepts of content writing. For content to be relevant to search engines, it must meet certain conditions such as the length of the content, the density of keywords (for some search engines that still take this notion into account), the internal network, etc. In 2012, in a study by serpIQ (whose site no longer exists), it was demonstrated that a web page containing more than 2,000 words often ranks in the top 10 of search results, or even in position 1 or 2, compared to pages that have less (see Figure 4.7).

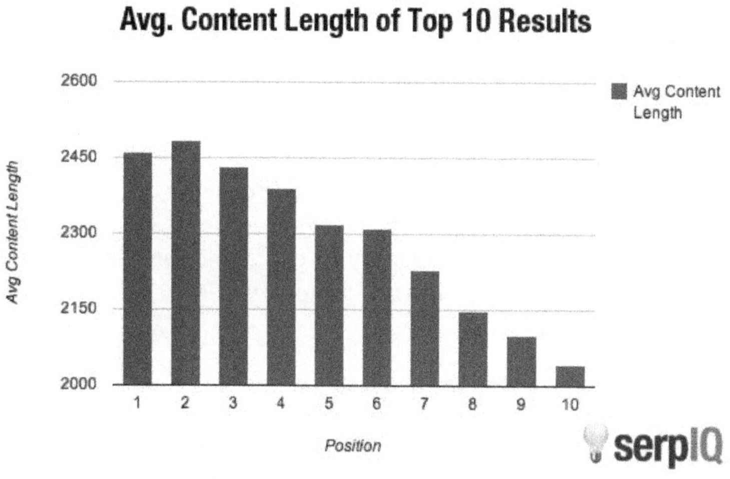

Figure 4.7. *Content length and impact on SEO positions per serpIQ[3]*

Content with more than 1,200 words sends a positive signal to Google and content with nearly 2,000 words sends a very good quality signal to

3 "Length of textual content", available at: https://searchengineland.com/seo-user-science-behind-long-form-content-230721.

Google. The idea is also to produce quality content that provides educational and unique information to Internet users.

For Asian languages, especially Chinese on Baidu, it is necessary to have articles of 1,000 Chinese characters, with about 15 or 20 keywords in the text; this represents approximately 2% of keyword density, since Baidu still takes into account this notion related to density.

For all search engines, when we are looking to optimize content, it is better to insert keywords at the beginning of articles, in the first paragraph for example, so that web crawlers see them immediately when they arrive and crawl the pages.

To optimize textual content, it is necessary to structure it with the heading titles tags (which we have seen earlier in this chapter) and to develop ideas in a clear way to have a hierarchy of information:

– H1: large general topic;

– H2: major theme;

– H3: category;

– H4 : subcategory;

– H5: product;

– H6: particularities of a product, element or concept.

Within the texts, it is also necessary to put in internal links that point to other pages on the site. We discuss this topic in section 4.6.

4.6. Optimization of internal network size

Internal network is a concept that can be summarized as the relationship between the internal pages of the website. The more internal links a page has (especially the home page, since it links all the pages together from itself), the more likely it is to be well positioned in search engines.

This is why it is important not to leave isolated pages (orphaned) and to try to link them together as much as possible (e.g. create a section of similar products to strengthen the internal network of the pages).

When we write articles, we always place links to internal pages on one or two keywords (text anchors that can be generic words, a product or brand name) in order to increase the visibility of all pages within the site. Ideally, new internal pages (such as news pages) should also be placed on the home page of the site, so that they can be indexed more quickly.

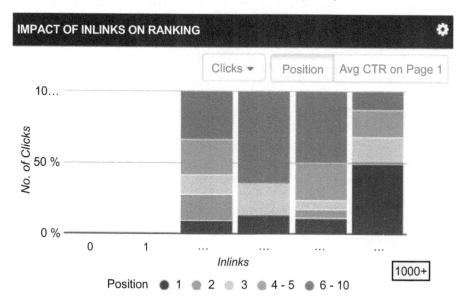

Figure 4.8. *The more inlinks (internal links) a page has, the more likely it is to be ranked at the top of the search results. For a color version of this figure, see www.iste.co.uk/duong/SEO1.zip*

When the internal network of the site is done well, all the site pages are indexed in search engines. It is necessary to avoid orphan pages because they can send a bad signal of a non-structure website to search engines.

Figure 4.9 provides an example of optimized content with internal links to other pages on the site.

Once all pages are properly linked together, with quality internal links, we estimate that 90% of the text content is optimized. There are still alt attributes to optimize and text anchors for breadcrumbs, internal and external links.

SEO #Naver : Zones stratégiques et Outils en #SEO Coréen

Bonjour tout le monde !

Récemment, j'ai répondu à des questions sur Twitter que les confrères SEO tels qu'Olivier Andrieu m'ont posées sur le SEO en Asie, et je réalise que mes deux articles précédents portent sur le SEO japonais sur Yahoo! Japan et le SEO russe sur Yandex, et je me suis dit que je pourrais regrouper ce que je sais sur le SEO coréen sur Naver ici.

Voici les tweets en question sur le SEO Naver et le SEO Baidu :

Veronique Duong ✿◉●•ⁱᵒ
@veroduong

Je faisais référence à la description mais la méta keywords a encore un impact sur le #SEO #Naver (Naver recommande de la remplir "avec quelques mots-clés séparés par des virgules")

O.Andrieu Abondance @abondance_com
En réponse à @veroduong

Description ou Keywords ?

♡ 2   19:57 - 28 nov. 2018

Figure 4.9. *Internal links (green boxes) to other articles (web pages) on the site. For a color version of this figure, see www.iste.co.uk/duong/SEO1.zip*

4.7. Optimization of alt attributes for images

In Chapter 3, we saw that alt attributes allow us to give an alternative textual description to images. It is important to put keywords in these alt attributes, so that the visuals can be correctly displayed in Google Images, Baidu Tupian, Yandex Images, etc.

The context around the image is also important. It is necessary to place captions, explanatory texts also containing keywords, so that the image has a better chance of being correctly displayed in image engines.

The alt attributes of images are to be optimized, especially for e-commerce sites selling products that must be well referenced.

Figure 4.10 provides an example of sites with empty alt attributes for product images.

Figure 4.10. *Empty alt attributes for product images*

By failing to fill in the alt attributes, there is a real loss of revenue for the SEO of images.

In addition, in Figure 4.10, we see that there is no textual content around product images. This makes it difficult for search engines to understand what types of products are involved, to categorize them correctly and to trace them back to relevant keywords.

Figure 4.11 provides an example of products with well optimized alt attributes.

Figure 4.11. *Product images with optimized alt attributes filled with unique information for each product*

When a site has a large volume of product pages, we propose to set up an automatic rule to systematically optimize alt attributes.

The alt attribute format we recommend is:

PRODUCT NAME - SEARCHED KEYWORD (from a study of keywords) - Brand

With this format, we have all the elements concerning the product and a keyword searched in the alt attributes.

For strategic images of the site, it is preferable to fill in the attributes manually in order to have full control over the optimization of the content for these visuals. It is also possible to follow the previous format for the manual filling of alt attributes.

Once the alt attributes of the images are filled in, it is estimated that the semantic content of the web page is 92% optimized.

To finalize semantic optimizations, we will discuss in the following sections the optimization of breadcrumb text anchors, internal link anchors and external links, and finally media files.

4.8. Optimization of breadcrumbs (anchors)

Breadcrumbs are central for navigating a site. They make it possible to strengthen a website's internal network and allow Internet users to understand where they are within the site. Breadcrumbs are like a path (see Figure 4.12).

... > DIVER 300 M > COLLECTION HOMME > 210.30.42.20.01.001

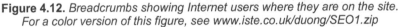

Figure 4.12. *Breadcrumbs showing Internet users where they are on the site. For a color version of this figure, see www.iste.co.uk/duong/SEO1.zip*

However, the breadcrumb problem in Figure 4.12 concerns the fact that the anchor of the product page is composed only of numbers (the product reference in this case) and this is not optimal for the site's internal network size in terms of text anchoring.

It is preferable to have a keyword in this area. We suggest for this example: "steel watch 210.30.42.20.01.001". Thus, we have a keyword that is "steel watch", followed by the reference number. If it is possible to add the name of the product, that can also be an interesting choice.

Text anchors can significantly improve the positioning of a page in search engines. The more clear and composed of relevant keywords, the more opportunities the page will have to rank them in search engines. Here is an ideal breadcrumb according to our recommendations:

Home > Category (search keyword) > Subcategory (search keyword) > Product (with keyword)

In order to have keywords in the breadcrumb, you must name the items in the menu with search terms (see the keyword study). Thus, when automatically retrieving data to compose the breadcrumb, the elements (categories, subcategories, products) will be systematically placed. Figure 4.13 provides an HTML source code where we can see how the breadcrumb is composed.

```
<div id="breadcrumbs">
    <div class="breadcrumbs" itemscope itemtype="http://data-vocabulary.org/Breadcrumb">
    <a style="text-decoration: underline;" itemprop="url" href="http://autoveille.free.fr">  <span itemprop="title">Accueil</span> </a>
        </div>
    <div class="breadcrumbs" itemscope itemtype="http://data-vocabulary.org/Breadcrumb">
>   <a style="text-decoration: underline;" itemprop="url" href="http://autoveille.free.fr/recherche-developpement-intelligence-artificielle.html" >
        </div>
    <div class="breadcrumbs" itemscope itemtype="http://data-vocabulary.org/Breadcrumb">
>   <a style="text-decoration: underline;" itemprop="url" href="http://autoveille.free.fr/definition-n-gramme.html" >  <span itemprop="title">Défini
        </div>
</div>
```

Figure 4.13. *Optimized breadcrumb HTML source code optimized with schema:org. For a color version of this figure, see www.iste.co.uk/duong/SEO1.zip*

The textual elements on a web page are important and we recommend optimizing them systematically in order to obtain an SEO-friendly page.

4.9. Optimization of internal and external anchors

The anchors of internal and external links need to be optimized, in order to send the right signals to search engines and make them "understand", based on which key terms we want to bring web pages up.

In Google Search Console, for example, it is possible to see the words on which external sites anchor text the most (see Figure 4.14).

Links > **Top linking text**

Top linking text ⑦	
↓ **Rank**	Link text
25	http veronique duong com
24	referencement analyse optimisation site internet
23	referencement optimisation site internet agence referencement lyon
22	italie du sud en camping car référencement généraliste et thématique sur votre site internet veille mediaveille
21	où trouver une agence de référencement google
20	lyon agence internet référencement gratuit
19	amputé 4 membres référencement généraliste et thématique sur votre site internet veille mediaveille
18	more veronique duong com

Figure 4.14. *Anchoring texts for external links in Google Search Console*

The anchors of external links have a considerable influence in relation to the positioning of web pages (use of strategic keywords required). If we want to go back to a searched keyword, we must use it as anchor text within the site and outside the site, on other external sites.

In Figure 4.14, we see that the anchors used on external sites refer to the first and last name of the author of this book, as well as her area of expertise (which is SEO).

By being precise in internal and external anchors (we often have to contact the owners of external sites to ask them to use a text anchor appropriate in relation to our activity), we send the right information to search engines and they better understand on which terms they should categorize and move the site up.

Following the optimization of internal and external anchors within and outside the site (we will come back to this topic in Chapter 5 on link building), we can finalize our semantic optimizations within the site, with the optimization of file names.

4.10. Media file optimization

Often omitted, the names of audio, video and image media files are important to optimize. Even if they have little influence for SEO, it is necessary to have a certain homogeneity in the site content.

The file names of images, videos and soundtracks must be optimized, and to do this it is possible to follow this format:

– image: product name-keywords-brand.jpg;

– video: product name-keywords-brand.mp4;

– audio: soundtrack-keywords-brand.mp3.

Accented and/or special characters should not be added to file names, as they are also file URLs. We remind the reader that URLs must not contain accented characters or special characters.

Here are some other rules to follow for file names:

– quotation marks replace spaces;

– the following characters are reserved for specific uses and therefore cannot be used in the URL: # $% & '() * +, / :; = ? @ [ ];

– uppercase letters should be avoided for URLs, as they are case sensitive (and few Internet users enter their URLs in upper case).

In order to avoid common errors when recovering files, special characters must also be removed when saving files.

In addition, it is not recommended to use circumflex accents in file names (â, ê, î, ô, û, etc.).

This editorial part is important, because it is part of one of the pillars of search marketing, and it is the optimized content that will allow a site to position itself and move up correctly in the search engines.

Following Chapters 3 and 4 on technical and semantic referencing, which constitute 50% of SEO pillars, we will discuss in Chapter 5 the main link building techniques, which consist in searching for external links to point to the main site to optimize.

## 5

Link-building Methods

Link building is one of the main pillars of SEO. Technical and semantic elements are important for the life and health of the site itself, but the external environment of the site also counts to make it efficient and gain visibility on the Web.

The objective of link-building strategies can be explained by this definition that we often give to our customers:

"The idea is to collect as many external links as possible, and of high quality, on reference sites and media. It is the latter that constitutes all the popularity of the website (nearly 50%). It is necessary to collect as many as possible, in order to start to rank the site well based on interesting keywords, thanks to the relevant external text anchors".

As per our experience, there are ten points to check to see if external links are of good quality:

– the PageRank of the page (Google no longer updates this index but still uses it, as do other search engines such as Baidu);

– domain names that point to the site;

– the domain authority;

– trust flow (trust site index, the existing index for Google, Baidu and Yandex, for example);

– links in textual contexts (and not present in footers, menus, etc.);

– the number of outgoing links from the external site (having a certain number of them can dilute its link strength);

– the relevance of the domain names to which the site is linked;

– the keywords of the text anchors;

– the co-citations;

– the preference for "dofollow" links, not "nofollow" (the dofollow attribute represents almost all the power of the link juice).

In the following sections, we will explain the main methods for searching for external links, as well as the advice we have tested and which works for collecting links from external sites.

There are various practices, more or less compliant with search engines, used by different types of SEO consultants (black hat SEO, gray hat SEO, etc.). Our objective is to communicate the most sustainable solutions (which are part of the white hat SEO) in relation to other competing sites and ethics.

5.1. Guest blogging

Guest blogging is one of our recommended methods to find external links, the objective being to write a guest article on another owner's blog and insert a link to one's own site in the article. This technique is often free of charge, as it consists of a fair exchange of items or other online promotional services.

This can be done in the form of interviews, expert articles on a specific subject, etc. In the field of SEO, guest blogging is a common practice and a method that works to obtain external links that point to the site concerned.

The person who most often writes the article in the case of guest blogging is the invited person themself. The person who invites reads the article again. And if it suits them, they put the article online or plan to put it online in the next few days, weeks or even in the months to come (often a publication schedule exists for bloggers specialized in guest blogging).

The author of this book herself tested the guest blogging format and gave interviews on other SEO blogs (see Figure 5.1).

Véronique nous parle dans cette belle interview de son parcours professionnel, de sa passion pour le SEO, son rôle et ses objectifs en tant que présidente de l'association et surtout de l'événement SEO de l'année : le SEO Campus Paris le 22 & 23 mars prochains ! On se retrouve là-bas ? ☺

Bonne découverte !

Questions sur Véronique, la femme

Qui est Véronique Duong ?

Véronique Duong est une **jeune femme dynamique,** qui déborde d'énergie positive, et qui est passionnée par beaucoup d'activités dans la vie, dont le SEO (depuis 2010 / 2011) !

Aujourd'hui, je suis **entrepreneure** (directrice de Rankwell, agence SEO internationale) et **auteure** (depuis 2017), et ce sont les deux plus belles choses qui sont arrivées dans ma carrière professionnelle pour le moment !

• Raconte-nous un peu ton parcours professionnel

Je suis diplômée d'un Master 2 en ingénierie linguistique / traitement automatique des langues, et je suis **ingénieure linguiste** (TAListe) de formation. Comme j'ai appris en formation à coder

Figure 5.1. *Expert interview with the author of this book on the blog of another SEO consultant (in French). For a color version of this figure, see www.iste.co.uk/duong/SEO1.zip*

We note in the article the presence of relevant keywords such as *parcours professionel* ("professional background"), *entrepreneure* ("entrepreneur"), *ingénieure linguiste* ("computational engineer") and *auteure* ("author"). It is on these terms that you must place a link (hyperlink type) to the site to be optimized. The link to the external site must be placed at the top of the page.

The ideal length for a guest article is approximately 800 words. Thus, search engines will see a good code/text ratio signal and the external link to the site to be optimized will be less "visible", at first sight, to Internet users and crawlers.

In section 5.2, we will take a look at paid external publications, a practice that is often controversial but which works well if everything is under control.

5.2. Paid external publications

The objective of paid external publications via specialized platforms is to pay for an article or to pay for the possibility of having a link to the site to be optimized on another owner's site.

Costs vary greatly from one site to another, as the business model on this point is not yet clear, and there are no standards or regulations on the subject at the time of writing.

A referencing paid article and a link to the site to be made visible can cost anything from 20 euros to more than 2,000 euros, depending on the site's metrics: is its domain authority powerful? Is its trust flow index sufficient? Is its citation flow in other sites satisfactory?

All these questions must be asked to make sure that the purchase of the item we are buying is a wise choice.

As soon as we find an interesting paid article, we carry out the transaction on the publication platform. Then the owner of the site will be responsible for making an article including a link to the website to be optimized.

Once this action is carried out on the owner's side, we can consider that they have made an external link to our site.

We have spoken about terms such as trust flow, citation flow and domain authority. Here are their definitions, according to Majestic[1], the entity that proposed the following terms.

– *Trust flow*: to define a reliable trust index for each URL, Majestic used a high volume list of manually analyzed sites that met the trust criteria common to all search engines (e.g. Dmoz and Yellowpages).

The list is not exhaustive, but it is significant enough according to Majestic for their algorithms and calculations to be reliable on a Web scale. The trust flow is therefore calculated from link to link, from the outgoing links of the sites in the list. It symbolizes the ability of a page to convey a good reputation and trust.

---

1 "Bien comprendre les Flow Metrics de Majestic SEO" (translation: Definitions of Trust Flow and Citation Flow according to Majestic), available at: https://blog.majestic.com/fr/developpement/flow-metrics-2/ (in French).

– *Citation flow*: metrics that indicate the popularity of the page, an evaluation of its ability to transmit link juice power. This figure is calculated from the total number of links, the number of reference domains, etc. It is graduated from 0 to 100: the higher the citation flow of a page, the more popularity it is able to achieve.

– *Domain authority (concept initiated by MOZ, an independent company specialized in search in the United States)*: the domain authority evolves on a scale from 1 to 100: the higher the score for a domain authority, the more powerful it is considered as a domain in the eyes of crawlers (GoogleBot, BaiduSpider, etc.). It takes into account the number and quality of incoming links or backlinks to the domain name, as well as other factors related to site referencing such as content or traffic.

Publishing external articles (free or paid guest blogging) on powerful reference sites is a method that we recommend, because it is a clean practice, where the website link to be optimized is contextualized, which will send an even better signal to search engines.

There are other methods that provide even more links and we will explore them in the following sections.

5.3. Link ninja

There is a method for collecting external links called *link ninja*. The purpose of this practice is to request links directly from webmasters of other sites and to place these links in the footers, menus and home page of a site.

The process consists of finding a site on which to place the link to the website to be optimized, then putting this link there and hoping that it is validated by the webmaster who manages the site.

It is a tedious practice that generates few returns on investment. We will provide the methodology of the strategy, but we do not recommend focusing all your efforts on this strategy.

Often, links are obtained by commenting on blog posts, posting in forums or by sending a request to a webmaster of the specialized site on which we want to display the link of the site to be optimized.

Figure 5.2 shows an example of a possible link ninja (comment under an article, with the brand of the site to be optimized as an anchor that links to the site's home page).

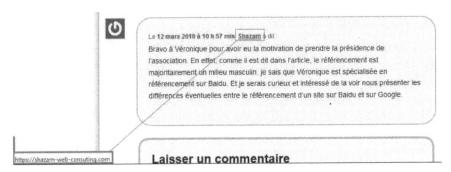

Figure 5.2. *Comment with the name of the site to be optimized as an anchor, referring to the site's home page in question*

This link ninja method is time consuming and generates few results. It should be used in a secondary way, when time or resources permit.

In the following section, we will discuss another practice known in the world of SEO. This is link baiting (or inbound marketing).

5.4. Link baiting (inbound marketing)

The objective of link baiting (or inbound marketing because, in our opinion, both terms are synonymous) is to create quality content on a site to be optimized and ensure that this content naturally attracts other webmasters from other sites to make links to ours.

In terms of content, we will not only focus on articles and text content. In the case of link baiting, we are talking about multimedia content, games, contests, quizzes and different formats that encourage Internet users to come to the site to be optimized and share this content with their networks via their sites, which in turn will share information equally. Informative and educational computer graphics are also a good way to promote a site. A relevant and concrete image is worth more than a piece of text in certain areas and, if it arouses interest, this image will be actively shared among Internet users.

At a time when photos and visual content are popular on social networks, and easier to read on mobile devices, it is interesting to focus on this point.

Figure 5.3. *Presentation graphics[2] of the author of this book. For a color version of this figure, see www.iste.co.uk/duong/SEO1.zip*

We wish to remind you that each graphic or visual must be accompanied by relevant text and context (with an optimized alt attribute) so that the image can be quickly indexed in search engines ("Images" section) and that

2 "Infographie de présentation de Véronique Duong", available at: https://autoveille.files. wordpress.com/2018/ 07/infographie_veronique_duong_jul_2018.jpg (in French)

it can be used both in SEO images and in social networks such as Instagram, Pinterest, etc.

The author of this book, to introduce herself and explain her activities, presents computer graphics on her blog that summarize her background and her main occupations (see Figure 5.3).

An informative computer graphic or a visual is much more concrete than a text and arouses more desire to share with Internet users. However, as mentioned above, any image must be accompanied by context in order to properly optimize it. Often, it is not the computer graphics alone (the.jpg or.png) that is shared, but the entire web page, including the text article. That is why it must be well written and optimized in SEO, with relevant text anchors.

The idea of link baiting is to create interactive and viral content, which arouses the interest of Internet users to share information and learn more about a brand, an entity or a person.

We have talked about textual content, articles and computer graphics, but videos are also an interesting format to generate interest. Again, it is necessary to accompany these context videos, so that they can be correctly uploaded in SEO Videos (Google Videos, Baidu Shipin, etc.).

Many ideas exist and it is necessary to let imagination, innovation and creativity be expressed in the case of the link baiting.

In section 5.5, we will discuss other practices and methods to create more presence on the Web and ensure a certain visibility for a brand or site.

5.5. Product tests or services

Having a product or service tested free of charge (in exchange for an external link) is a good way to showcase your know-how. This method is known in the influencer world, but it also exists in SEO.

If the site to be optimized in question is an e-commerce site, it would be very interesting for the site owner to have one of their products tested by leading bloggers in the field and to create a link to their site, where the bloggers will write an article to explain the product, give their opinions, etc.

If the site to be made more visible is a showcase site for service delivery, it is just as relevant to have the services tested by bloggers, partners, etc., and to ask them to talk about them on their blogs or sites, in the form of articles with links that point to the initial showcase site.

These are methods that require products and services that generate interest, but they work with all sectors. However, it is necessary to find bloggers and Internet users interested in the product or service in order to have them test and write about them.

These methods also encourage people to talk about an event. In Figure 5.4, we provide an example of an SEO event to which we were invited and about which we subsequently wrote an article, mentioning the name of the event.

Retour sur le We Love SEO 2018 @OnCrawl_FR @WeLoveSEO18

Bonjour tout le monde !

Dans cet article, je vous livre mon avis sur le We Love SEO 2018 qui a été une très bonne édition selon moi, avec des conférences très intéressantes ! Je suis restée, pour une fois, du début à la fin à un événement SEO sans avoir à courir à droite à gauche. Au début, je vous avoue que je ne voulais rester que la matinée car j'avais pas mal de réunions, mais voyant le déroulé de la journée, j'ai commencé à déplacer tous mes rendez-vous pour rester au We Love SEO ! Vous vous rendez compte ?! 😊

J'arrive pile poil au moment où la conférence sur le Crawl Budget a commencé, et heureuse de ne pas l'avoir loupé (j'aurais été verte) ! En résumé, cette dernière portait sur la gestion et l'optimisation du maillage interne, le robots.txt, le sitemap.xml, et comment faire pour que Google ne découvre que des pages d'informations intéressantes et faire indexer ces dernières qui peuvent être très volatiles (ex : offres d'emploi).

Les conseils donnés étaient très intéressants, mais pour un public un peu débutant, cela aurait été trop technique. Je vous mets les photos et mon live tweet de la conf ci-dessous :

Figure 5.4. *Article about being a guest of an SEO event, mentioning the name of the activity (in French)*

In Figure 5.5, we also propose another example, where we tested a log analysis tool for free and wrote an article mentioning the brand that allowed us to test the platform.

Test de l'outil d'analyse de logs gratuit (open source) d'OnCrawl (ELK)

Hello tout le monde,

Pendant l'été, j'ai eu un peu de temps pour tester quelques outils SEO, et celui que je vais vous présenter aujourd'hui est l'analyseur de logs open source d'OnCrawl. Je vous préviens dès maintenant qu'il faut avoir quelques compétences de développement et maîtriser à minima les lignes de commande (shell), sinon vous n'allez pas vous en sortir.

Il y a un guide d'installation tout prêt ici : Guide facile : Comment installer l'Analyseur de Logs Open Source d'OnCrawl

Mais je vais vous refaire les step by step avec mes mots et mes images 🙂

1. J'ai téléchargé Docker Toolbox
2. J'ai installé la Virtual Machine (VM) qui va avec
3. J'ai lancé le terminal de Docker pour faire fonctionner la commande *docker-compose -f docker-compose.yml up -d*

Figure 5.5. *Article written by the author on testing the tool offered by the mentioned entity and including a link to their site (boxed text) (in French)*

The methods of testing products or services as well as invitations to events work very well if the target is well defined.

We can get a free product or service in exchange for an external link on our blog or website. It is a way of generating content, interest and visibility for our site and for the external partner's site.

In the following sections, we provide additional ideas on how to create content and interactions external to your site, which still allow you to write relevant articles with a link to your site to be optimized.

5.6. Participation in events

Participating in trade fairs, conferences, seminars, meetings, etc. in order to promote brand or website awareness is a good way to make yourself visible to other actors, companies and entities in a sector.

To do this, it is necessary to constantly monitor and actively participate in events in the sector in question, to create recurrences and meetings with other organizations, and thus make a name for yourself little by little.

After participating in these events, the best way to maintain your visibility is to talk about this event and mention the entity organizing the event in an article, on a blog or in a news section of the site, hoping that the latter shares the article that mentions it to its network.

If this works, the beginning of the visibility of the new brand or site can be achieved. This operation must be repeated for all events in which a brand or company participates.

Figure 5.6 shows an example of an article we wrote after participating in an event (meetup) that the entity then shared on its network.

Résumé et retour d'expérience du Meetup @Botify sur « SEO & Publishers – Qualité des contenus »

Bonjour tout le monde !

Si vous êtes sur Twitter et faites votre veille informationnelle en SEO intensément, vous auriez dû voir que Botify a organisé un meetup sur la qualité des contenus SEO récemment, et j'ai participé à cet événement en tant que Speaker. Sur leur site, ou plutôt leur blog, ils ont fait un excellent résumé du meetup ... et j'ai été cité à plusieurs reprises. Merci pour cela Botify !

Vous trouverez l'article de Botify sur leur blog officiel : SEO & Publishers: Meetup Highlights

Voici quelques citations de Botify (c'est en anglais dans l'article, mais le meetup était en français) :

BOTIFY   HOME   FEATURES   PRICING   SUPPORT   BLOG   LOG IN

Here are some of the highlights of Botify Meetup #4: SEO & Publishers:

On managing content quality:

"For AuFeminin, as a pure-player, SEO is our entire history. We work with journalists who are trained daily in SEO." - Claire Sassonia

"You must not write just to write. You have to write to say something to generate quality traffic." - Veronique Duong

"Content is updated and follows trends. We watch what works and what doesn't work, and then we try something new." - Charlotte Prevost

"[For us] it requires at least 800 words to generate traffic. The more words in the articles, the more traffic they generate. I found this through using Botify... But, at the same time, equally

Figure 5.6. *Article on a meetup in which we participated, the entity mentioning our name in its own article*

Because of this method, our name is visible to Internet users, and especially to other specialists in our field, who will then be able to talk about us to other entities.

Participating in events as a speaker or contributor requires patience because to be selected you often already need to have a reputation. Events generally choose well-known personalities to attract more participants. We therefore offer another way to participate in events when we have a new brand: event sponsorship.

Becoming a sponsor at events related to the specific themes of our sector can be an interesting solution when we are a new brand. We have a case study to propose, because at the time of writing this book we are running a new SEO agency, created less than a year ago. So it is a new brand that no one knows about.

This is why we decided to become a sponsor of a well-known event in the SEO sector in order to give visibility to this new brand.

The event's Twitter account created a dedicated publication on social networks, with our logo and a link to our entity's account (see Figure 5.7).

Figure 5.7. *Sponsor an event to create visibility for a new brand*

Finding ideas to increase brand visibility involves active searching and long-term monitoring that in turn requires imagination, creativity and patience. There are a multitude of methods and it is up to us to exploit them, test them, invest time and measure the return on investment. If a method works, it is necessary to focus on it, while keeping an eye on other possible solutions.

In section 5.7, we will discuss the point of viral videos, which can effectively promote a new brand or website.

5.7. Video marketing

With the rise of mobile devices, which have become a must in terms of usage and navigation, the video format is a good practice to adopt to promote a company's products and services through interaction. Several e-commerce sites present their products with short videos that show the product from all angles (360°). It also allows Internet users to fully understand how the product works and how to use it.

It should be noted that tutorial videos are of great interest because they inform and teach Internet users and mobile users how the products work.

When an individual feels like learning new techniques for professional or personal use, it is a real bonus for the brand or website, because the user will remember the video that helped him/her.

For example, the site presented in Figure 5.8 invites us to watch the video of its new product with a call to action: "Regarder le film" (watch the movie).

Figure 5.8. *Call to action to view the video on the new product on the website*

On a mobile device (smartphone, tablet or other), the video format will take over the entire screen and present the product in such a way that the user finds it interesting to acquire it. Calls to action, keywords and text content around and in the video will play an important role in engaging Internet users to share and communicate about the brand, video and product.

For a site that sells services or a personality that offers expertise services, video is also a reliable way to present and make a brand or person popular.

In the case of a brand that offers services, it is necessary to create an introductory video on the brand and a video on each service offered. Each video should only talk about one topic (similar to a web page, which only addresses one topic per page).

For example, in Figure 5.9 displaying a company's YouTube channel, we can note that the brand has created different sections (events, TV ads, reports, etc.) to categorize videos about carpooling services.

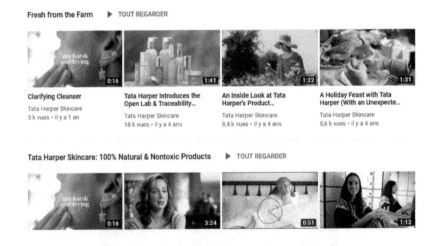

Figure 5.9. *Categorization of videos with specific themes*

The brand has a wide range of video content to promote its services in different settings: events, reports, advertisements, testimonials, etc.

In the case of a personality who offers services (such as a doctor, a lawyer or an expert in a field), it is interesting to make videos by theme, and in particular recorded interviews.

For interviews, the most interesting thing is to be interviewed by a well-known actor in the field, because he or she will also be able to share the video on online spaces. It is also relevant to film tutorials, explanatory videos and training courses in order to consolidate the expertise of the services.

Figure 5.10 shows examples, by the author of this book, who gave interviews with well-known actors in the SEO field.

Figure 5.10. *Interviews given in the form of exchanges, tutorials and webinars by the author of the book to a multinational entity known in the field of SEO and online marketing*

By working with recognized organizations in a field, it is possible to quickly gain reputation and visibility. Internet users who view the videos, if they find them relevant, will share them with their networks, and this will create external links and increase visibility. It is necessary to maintain a certain pace of content creation. For articles, we recommend creating one at least once a week (or, if resources are limited, once every 2 weeks). For computer graphics, we recommend at least once every 2 or 3 months, and for videos, about once or twice every semester.

We also use yet another way to create visibility for a new brand: the press reviews we publish in leading and national media.

5.8. Writing press reviews

In addition to all the points mentioned above, we can complete our strategy with publications in the reference media. We call this digital press relations. Often, for this task, we rely on a press expert, such as a press officer for example.

The objective is to produce press releases on a new product, a new event, a new book, etc., and to offer them to different media referents. Some well-known French reference media, such as *Les Échos* or *Le Journal du Net* (*Le Figaro* group), make it possible to create expert forums and publish them (subject to validation by the reference media).

We have published articles and columns in the leading French and Canadian reference media.

Figure 5.11 is an example of a Canadian radio podcast (interview given by the author of the book), accompanied by a textual article to optimize the indexing of the article.

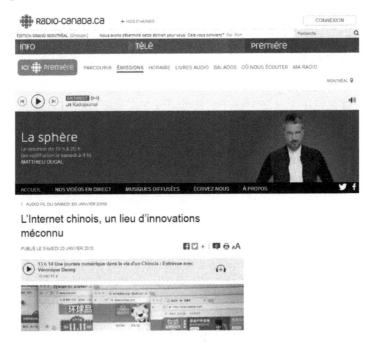

Figure 5.11. *Radio program* La Sphère *on* Ici Radio Canada Première: *"L'Internet chinois, un lieu d'innovations méconnu"*[3]

---

3 "A digital day in the life of a Chinese person: interview with Véronique Duong", available at: https://ici.radio-canada.ca/premiere/emissions/la-sphere/segments/entrevue/55635/internet-chine-wechat-innovation-publicity (in French).

As mentioned above, it is also possible to provide forums or write columns on specific expertise topics for reference media, as in our example in Figure 5.12.

Figure 5.12. *Article published in* Les Échos: *"E-commerce chinois et SEO Baidu: les tendances actuelles", proposed by Véronique Duong and validated by* Les Échos[4]

Writing external publications on specific topics and expertise in national and international media helps to strengthen the online reputation of a brand, company or expert.

We recommend that most companies and entities use this digital press relations solution at least twice a year in order to maintain an expert brand image and a good reputation. Indeed, it sends a positive signal to search engines when they discover the brand's mention in influential reference media at the national or even international level.

In this chapter, we have presented various recommended, concrete means and solutions that should be implemented regularly to create visibility for a site or a brand and to collect external links.

The work of seeking external links and visibility to build a solid and sustainable reputation is a project to be carried out over the long term. As a

4 "E-commerce chinois et SEO Baidu : les tendances actuelles", available at: https://www. lesechos.fr/idees-debats/cercle/cercle-178171-e-commerce-chinois-et-seo-baidu-les-tendances-actuelles-2146450.php (in French)

result of our experience, we believe that only in this way can we measure the effectiveness of the solutions implemented in practice.

Once link building strategies are implemented and methods work by generating more organic traffic, more new site visits and more concrete conversions, we believe that the SEO campaign is properly implemented and that all we need to do is maintain our efforts, testing other online promotion solutions to always get more visibility (see Chapter 2, section 2.12, on KPI tracking).

In Chapter 6, we will discuss the scientific side of SEO by explaining some of the themes related to computational engineering.

## 6

Computational Engineering Applied to SEO

Let us start this chapter with a definition of computational engineering: it is a discipline that involves computer science being applied to natural language. This includes many professions related to translation, terminology, text search, opinion search, corpus work and search engine work.

When we talk about computational engineering, we often associate it with the field of natural language processing (NLP). If NLP were to be defined, we could say NLP is a field that combines linguists and computer scientists.

A dual skill is required, as NLP is based on both linguistic and computer skills. There are also formalisms, which are representations of information and knowledge in machine-readable formats (scripting languages, command lines, etc.) and which are very important to take into account.

6.1. Semantic ontologies

In computational engineering, ontologies are graphs that represent semantic relationships between concepts and themes.

An ontology is the structured set of terms and concepts representing the meaning of an information field, whether through the metadata of a namespace or through the elements of a knowledge domain.

Ontology itself is a data model that represents a set of concepts in a field, as well as the relationships between them.

Figure 6.1 provides an example of an ontology in the mountain bike field.

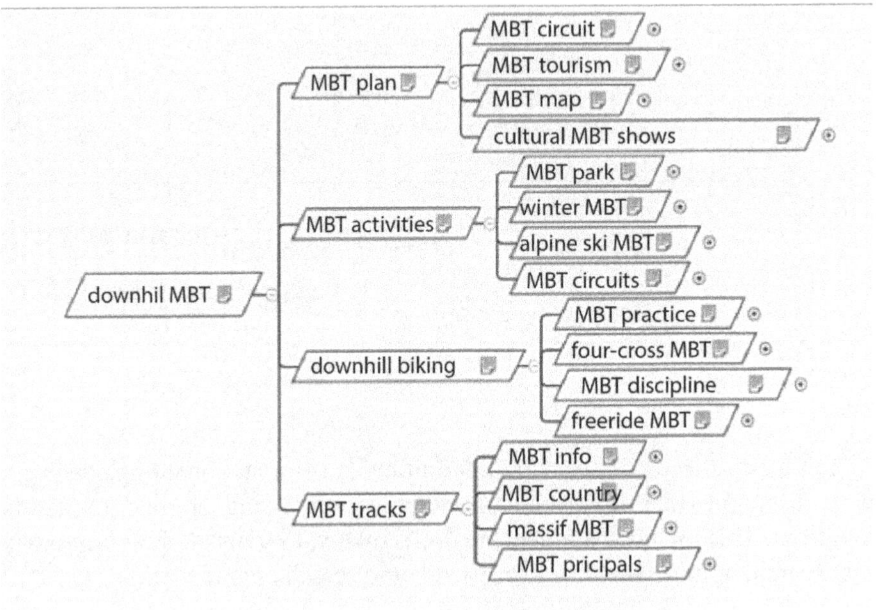

Figure 6.1. *Example of ontology, a graph of semantic relationships*

In SEO, we start from the most generic information to the most specific. When we need to establish a keyword study for a site, we start from its menu (often it contains the most generic terms) and, the more we go from categories to categories and subcategories to subcategories, the more specific concepts and elements we will have.

If the work of semantic relations between pages is not done, it is necessary to start it, because it is important for users, like for search engines, to see the precise themes of the site when they arrive on it.

Figure 6.2 represents an ontology that we created to semantically categorize and mesh the pages of a site with each other.

Ontology is done to describe the world as it is. Ontology seeks to formally describe a field of knowledge, identifying the types of objects in that field, their properties and relationships.

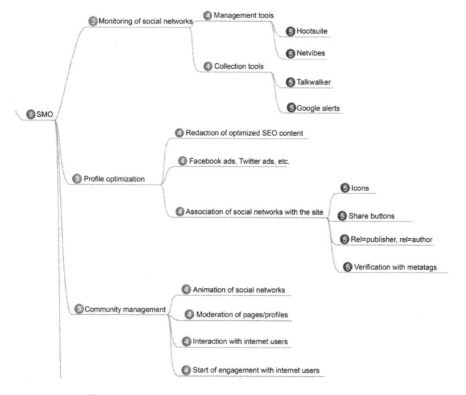

Figure 6.2. *Ontology for a social media optimization site*

In SEO, it is the ontologies that we use, because we are in a mode of "semantic relationships".

Figure 6.3 illustrates an example of an ontology where we see semantic links.

An internal semantic mesh between the pages (optimized internal anchors) will enable us to reach much more interesting semantic scores. We sometimes see confusion between ontologies and taxonomies.

Taxonomy refers to the classification of resources into files and categories. In other words, it refers to the "science of classification" and, by extension, any classification and categorization system.

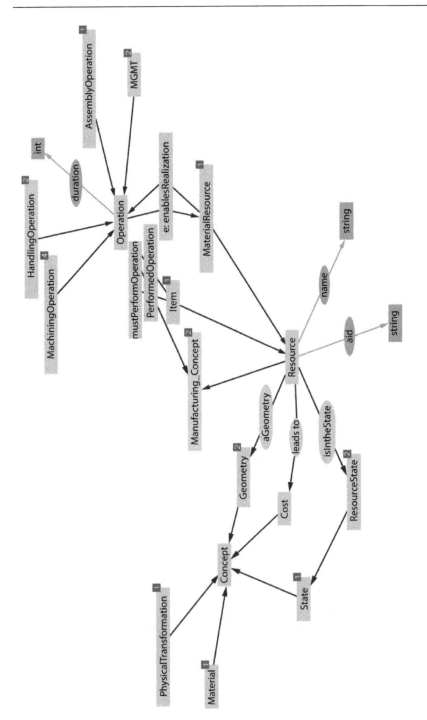

Figure 6.3. *Ontology with visualization of semantic relationships. For a color version of this figure, see www.iste.co.uk/duong/SEO1.zip*

Therefore, in SEO, taxonomies can help us to structure a site well, for example, by classifying the different pages at different levels. We are talking more about taxonomies than ontologies for classifying pages at different levels of depth (Home/Categories/Subcategories/Products/Articles, etc.).

We find that ontologies and taxonomies are two different concepts in linguistics, which can be interesting to apply in the field of SEO.

Speaking of semantic scores in the next section, we discuss the notion of term frequency-inverse document frequency (TF-IDF), a historical method created in the 1980s by researchers in language and information sciences.

6.2. TF-IDF

The TF-IDF is a historical method, founded in the 1980s, for implementing information search tools. The typical example to illustrate the TF-IDF measurement is the search engine, which must select the most relevant documents for a given query. A Boolean search in indexes gives a high volume of results, which are not ordered, and therefore it generates a lot of noise (we speak of "noise" when irrelevant answers are proposed by the database query system).

The TF-IDF algorithm addresses this defect by simultaneously exploiting the number of occurrences of terms (TF) and their semantic importance in the document collection (IDF) to order the results and present at the top of the list those that a simple statistical calculation tells us are the most relevant. Other algorithms are now more efficient, but this one remains the foundation, because it is very reliable, solid and stable: it can be easily implemented and constitutes an excellent starting point to measure the weight and presence of a keyword in a corpus of web pages.

The TF-IDF is implemented in many languages in the form of libraries (modules, scripts, computer packages) and requires very little programing for its implementation and limited resources (computing time or memory) when it is executed. Thus, when researchers in computational engineering work on projects for which they need results quickly and for which the requirements are not high in terms of relevance, the TF-IDF is appropriate.

If the requirements are higher, it is possible to use the TF-IDF as a reference point, before using other more sophisticated models, such as the LSA ("latent semantic analysis").

It should be noted, however, that the TF-IDF only uses the texts of the documents. This can be an advantage for documentary databases, but a disadvantage if links are made between documents (such as hyperlinks on the Web): they provide very important information, which will not be taken into account by the TF-IDF.

Here is an example of a concrete case study: a company that needs to set up an internal search engine with regard to its documents and wants to integrate it into its portal, but does not know which engine to choose. If a free solution should be recommended, it is possible to offer it at a preliminary stage easily and quickly: setting up a TF-IDF and allowing users to make their first requests, before analyzing the limitations of this first approach. Subsequently, depending on the feedback, it may be a priority to improve the internal search engine, but perhaps also to work on the quality of documents, the creation of adequate resources to improve searches, and implement other functionalities.

We find that the TF-IDF method remains effective and powerful in many cases. It is especially recommended to measure the presence of keywords in pages, and it is very popular in the field of text mining (text mining, a specialization of data mining on the Web and other media in the field of artificial intelligence).

When we talk about keywords, term weighting, co-occurrents and in texts, it is necessary to address the notion of n-grams and their usefulness.

6.3. N-grams

N-grams are sequences of words, strings of characters that follow each other and form word bags. We also talk about unigram, bigram or trigram.

Many SEO and automatic language processing tools use n-grams to detect duplicate content or repetitions.

Because of similar character sequences, robots and scripts can generate similarity scores between two web pages in terms of content.

The example in Figure 6.4 with the SEO tool shows a website's uniqueness in terms of its content.

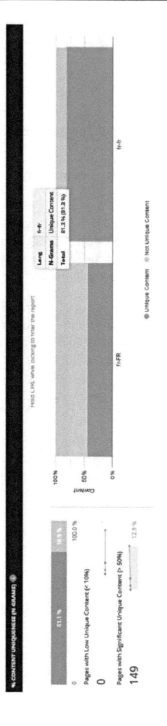

Figure 6.4. *Unicity of texts measured using n-grams.*
For a color version of this figure, see www.iste.co.uk/duong/SEO1.zip

In order to illustrate the n-grams in concrete terms, here is an example of splitting words into sequences based on the sentence "When the mystery is too overpowering, one dares not disobey":

– *word unigrams*: when/the/mystery/is/too/overpowering/one/dares/not/ disobey;

– *bigrams of words*: when the/the mystery/mystery is/is too/too overpowering/one dares/dares not/not disobey;

– *trigrams of words*: when the mystery/the mystery is/mystery is too/is too overpowering.

SEO and language engineering tools use n-grams and word sequences to measure whether the content is unique between site pages and so that there is no duplicate internal content (this can be detrimental to search engine algorithms, which seek uniqueness to offer Internet users).

Google also launched Ngram Viewer in 2010, a linguistic application that observed the change of frequency of one or more words or groups of words over time in printed sources (Google Books). In our opinion, it was a kind of Google Trend for books and sources in book format. However, the tool has not been updated since 2013.

Figure 6.5 provides an overview of Google Ngram Viewer.

After understanding how search engines weigh and report search results on a given query using the TF-IDF method and n-gram word sequences to detect duplicate content, we will discuss the subject of named entities, which hold an important role for the future in terms of knowledge graphs and voice searches.

6.4. Named entities

A named entity is a linguistic expression that refers to a name of a place, person or organization. Named entities are used in the field of automatic language processing or in the analysis of text corpora.

In the field of knowledge graphs, named entities are used by search engines to build elements of knowledge bases. We call these knowledge graphs.

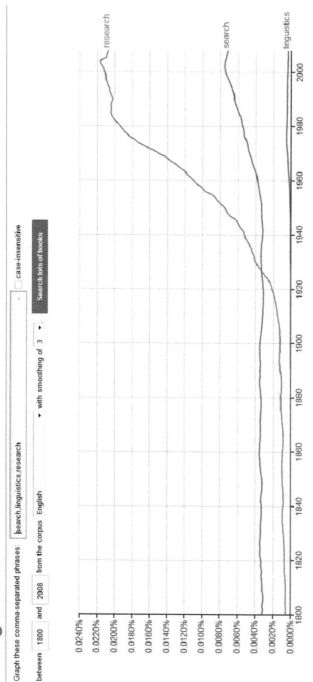

Figure 6.5. *Google Ngram Viewer. For a color version of this figure, see www.iste.co.uk/duong/SEO1.zip*

These graphs are used for voice search results in search engines that are trying to become response engines.

What is a knowledge graph?

A knowledge graph or knowledge base is the relationships that exist between the different named entities that are people, places and organizations.

Thanks to a properly trained knowledge graph, we can find very precise and direct answers to questions (queries) that we ask search engines.

Google tries with a large and robust knowledge graph to make the results smarter. Based on the pure semantic web, the graph helps users to have concrete summaries related to their search queries, such as biographies and event dates.

When we talk about named entities, the concept of name address phone (NAP) can be correlated on this subject. Knowledge graph data comes from "named entities".

There are language engineering tools available to label these terms, such as Unitex (see Figure 6.6).

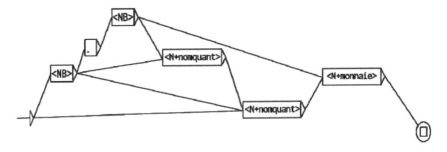

Figure 6.6. *Place, currency and population name labels in Unitex*

In the example in Figure 6.5, we performed our test on Chinese writing in Unitex. Here was the response: Unitex does not recognize Chinese characters and therefore most named entities (mainly proper names and place names) will have to be manually entered into the dictionary. The capacity of software to recognize Asian languages in NLP should be improved. Very often, the characters of Asian languages appear as squares because they are not recognized. However, we know that developing software for the automatic processing of European languages is already long, complex and costly to do.

To return to the subject of knowledge graphs, named entities are used by search engines to build elements of knowledge bases. These graphs are used for voice search results in search engines that are trying to become response engines.

Therefore, it is necessary to specify each time in the contents, and especially in the rich snippets, the names of the person (author), the place and the society in order to appear as precisely as possible in Google's knowledge graph.

In the following section, we give our point of view on the future of SEO coupled with the field of linguistic engineering.

6.5. SEO and computational engineering

In our experience, the future lies in voice search and voice response, with considerable progress in terms of human–machine communication and voice recognition.

Knowledge graphs make it possible to make the results of responses more and more accurate, and we now almost use a pure semantic web.

We will have to adapt to these new uses. In Asia, talking into your smartphone to carry out a search is already a normal activity. In Europe, the use is not yet widely adopted, but we estimate that from 2020 onwards, voice search will account for 70% of searches carried out (see Figure 6.7).

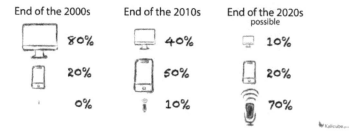

Figure 6.7. *From 2020, 70% of searches will be vocal (image source: Kalicube)*

In the short term, we will still see more or less strong developments with Google Home and other voice speakers, which are increasingly present on the market (for example in China with Baidu Xiaoyu or Tmall Genie X-1).

In Asia, AEO (Answer Engine Optimization) is already a habit (especially in China, which is one step ahead in terms of digital and artificial intelligence), while in the West, AEO is just arriving on the market with voice speakers.

In the long term, voice search will become a normal habit and will become part of our daily lives, as we have adapted by moving from VHS/K7 to DVD/MP3 and then from evolution to technological evolution.

Figures 6.8 and 6.9 represent the voice speakers of the two search engine giants, Google Home and Baidu Zaijia.

Figure 6.8. *Google Home*

Figure 6.9. *Baidu Xiaoyu Zaijia*

Technology is evolving and progressing at a constant and very fast pace around the world, and we must adapt to new uses. In SEO, we are the first to be concerned by these evolutions, because we work on websites and must always allow a brand to be visible on the Web.

We are among the pioneers in the work on voice search. This is why we conduct long-term research in order to successfully position the sites to be optimized at the top of written or oral research results.

This chapter on computational engineering and SEO aims to raise awareness among experts, referencing consultants, marketers and anyone interested in high technology and the new uses that are coming and will become part of our daily lives over time.

We must adapt and keep a constant eye on the latest developments in this sector. Artificial intelligence will play an important role in optimizing habits and uses and, in our opinion, it will remain an effective aid.

In Chapter 7, we will share our main tips on multilingual and international SEO, specifically on the following three search engines: Baidu, Yandex and Naver.

International SEO Specificities

Often, when we talk about SEO in the Western world, we are referring to that which is done in the case of Google. However, there are other local search engines that better meet market criteria.

Here are the most popular search engines by country, territory or region of the world:

– North America and Europe: Google, Bing;

– China: Baidu, Qihoo 360, Shenma (Alibaba), Sogou;

– South Korea: Sorry, Daum;

– France: Qwant;

– Japan: Yahoo! Japan;

– Czech Republic: Seznam;

– Russia: Yandex.

There are still other more secondary search engines such as Ask.com, AOL, DuckDuckGo, etc., but their market shares are often less than 2 or 3%.

In the remaining chapter, we will focus on the three main search engines other than Google: Baidu, Yandex and Naver.

7.1. Baidu SEO

Baidu is the top search engine used in China. It was created in 2000 by Robin Lin, an engineer. In 2018, Baidu had nearly 69.74% of the market share in China. The next most popular search engines are Qihoo 360, Shenma and Sogou. Google has almost no market share in China, with only 1.53%.

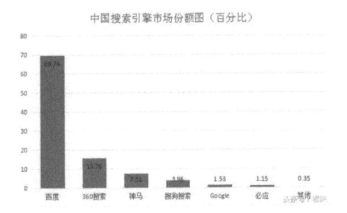

中国搜索引擎市场份额图（百分比）

Figure 7.1. *Market share of search engines in China in 2018*

To succeed in the SEO of your site on Baidu, the search engine on which we focus, there are several strategies, in addition to the classic SEO strategy, which perform audits, meta tag optimizations, technical optimizations, etc. Local, administrative and governmental criteria must be taken into account.

Here are our recommendations to have a good foundation in Baidu SEO:

– have a website fully adapted in simplified Chinese;

– have a .cn or.com domain;

– have accommodation in China or, if it is a foreign company in China, accommodation in Hong Kong;

– have a Chinese continental mobile line using +86 (Hong Kong using + 852 does not work for mobile lines, which are necessary for opening different accounts);

– have an ICP license validated by the Chinese government[1];

– have Baidu-specific accounts, such as Baidu Ziyuan, Baidu Tongji, Baidu Index and Baidu Passport;

1 Duong V., *Baidu SEO: Challenges and Intricacies of Marketing in China*, ISTE Press, London and John Wiley & Sons, New York, 2017; available at: http://iste.co.uk/book.php?id=1172.

– have V cards to reinforce the reputation and visibility of the site;

– have the "official website" icon in Chinese;

– have the "authenticated brand and logo" icon.

Figure 7.2 provides an example of a search result for a Chinese telephone brand.

Figure 7.2. *Baidu icons to build trust*

For websites connected to the tourism and travel sectors, it is also possible to include an airplane icon with the search result (see Figure 7.3).

Figure 7.3. *Airplane icon certifying the brand or travel agency*

Obtaining numerous opinions is also a strategy that can be adopted to gain visibility for the brand. The opinions are often read by Chinese internet users and make it possible to improve the reputation of a website. It should be noted that Baidu takes into account opinions for the SEO classification of a Chinese website.

The SEO criteria on Baidu are different from those of Google, because they take into account the social aspect and the external communication of the brand, such as the branding and the brand image.

The top 4 SEO criteria of Baidu are:

1) shares by users;

2) link building;

3) the brand's influence (branding, brand image) ;

4) opinions from SNS (social networks, BBS or Chinese forums).

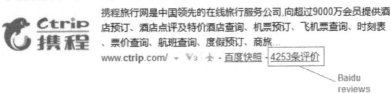

Figure 7.4. *Baidu opinion*

Baiduspider, which is Baidu's crawler, visits web pages daily to index them. But, in our experience, it is slower than GoogleBot to update its index.

Figure 7.5 illustrates how Baiduspider works.

Figure 7.5. *Funnel representing the functioning of Baiduspider. For a color version of this figure, see www.iste.co.uk/duong/SEO1.zip*

Here are the elements present in this funnel illustrating how Baidu scans a web page:

– red: browsing of the keyword database;

– blue: content and web page;

– green: crawl by Baiduspider;

– purple: page indexing;

– yellow: positioning of pages, then generation of SEO traffic.

Baidu believes that SEO can be summarized in the following three points:

1) The Internet user searches for information using Baidu, and Baidu returns answers corresponding to this search.

2) SEOs try to attract Internet users to their sites (with various SEO methods and tips).

3) Baidu users become the site's own users.

The diagram in Figure 7.6 shows the Chinese version of the three ideas above.

Figure 7.6. *Baidu's SEO strategy progression*

Baidu also separates the elements that transmit weight or not in terms of SEO in Figure 7.7.

Figure 7.7. *Elements having an impact in terms of SEO weight according to Baidu. For a color version of this figure, see www.iste.co.uk/duong/SEO1.zip*

Here are the elements that have an impact in terms of SEO (translation of the text to the left of the spider in Figure 7.7):

– internal mesh size;

– mobile-agent (sites adapted to mobile devices);

– optimized according to the guidelines;

– external links.

We note that internal and external links are very important to work on in order to create a solid base of links for Baidu.

Here are the elements that do not have a direct impact on SEO on Baidu (translation of the text located to the right of the spider in Figure 7.6):

– sitemap;

– ping (name of a computer command used to test the accessibility of another machine through an IP network);

– manual indexing.

Figure 7.8 illustrates an example of a ping.

The following is the output of running ping on Linux for sending five probes to the target host www.example.com:

```
$ ping -c 5 www.example.com
PING www.example.com (93.184.216.34): 56 data bytes
64 bytes from 93.184.216.34: icmp_seq=0 ttl=56 time=11.632 ms
64 bytes from 93.184.216.34: icmp_seq=1 ttl=56 time=11.726 ms
64 bytes from 93.184.216.34: icmp_seq=2 ttl=56 time=10.683 ms
64 bytes from 93.184.216.34: icmp_seq=3 ttl=56 time=9.674 ms
64 bytes from 93.184.216.34: icmp_seq=4 ttl=56 time=11.127 ms

--- www.example.com ping statistics ---
5 packets transmitted, 5 packets received, 0.0% packet loss
round-trip min/avg/max/stddev = 9.674/10.968/11.726/0.748 ms
```

Figure 7.8. *Examples of ping from Wikipedia*[2]

At the beginning of this book, we talked about Baidu MIP (Mobile Instant Pages), a new HTML language for alternative mobile versions, which is very clean and fast.

2 "Ping examples", available at: https://en.wikipedia.org/wiki/Ping_(networking_utility).

Many sites do not yet have MIP-friendly versions, but since we want brands to be pioneers in their fields, we recommend that they comply with Baidu MIP rules now.

Here is the specific markup in MIP language[3] (note that the markup is quite similar to Google AMP):

– start the HTML page with <!doctype html>;

– use the attribute "mip" in the html tag: <html mip>;

– use <head> and <body> ;

– in the <head> part, use the tag <meta charset="utf-8">, with utf-8 encoding only;

– in the <head> part, use the tag <meta name="viewport" content= "width=device-width,minimum-scale=1">, with this initial directive-scale=1;

– in the <head> part, use the tag < link rel="standardhtml" href= "xxx" >;

– in the <head> part, use < link rel="stylesheet" type="text/css" href= "https://mipcache.bdstatic.com/static/mipmain-v1.1.1.css" >;

– in the <body> part, use Javascript <script src= "https://mipcache. bdstatic.com/static/mipmain-v1.1.0.js" ></script >.

However, there are some tags that are prohibited in Baidu MIP language (see Figure 7.9).

frame	禁止使用	
frameset	禁止使用	
object	禁止使用	
param	禁止使用	
applet	禁止使用	
embed	禁止使用	
form	禁止使用	
input elements	禁止使用	包括 input, textareaa, select, option

Figure 7.9. *Tagging prohibited in Baidu MIP language*

3 "Official website of the MIP language (Baidu)", available at: https://www.mipengine.org.

Following the technical optimization of PC and/or mobile sites for Baidu, there are other strategies to protect site content and redirect pages that no longer exist using webmaster tools. Here are our recommendations.

Since August 2012, Baidu has been implementing a project that allows original authors to protect their content. This project against duplicate content is called Baidu Originality Meteor Program (百度原创星火计划) and it allows brands to protect their texts and articles.

The actions to be taken to protect content are as follows:

1) Information on the author(s), date and possible sources should be placed under H1 or H2 of the article (see Figure 7.10).

Figure 7.10. *Article with dates, first and last name of the author and category*

2) The following code must be included in the web pages to declare the authors:

```
// This is a mandatory and fixed entry

<meta property="og :type" content="article"/>

// The earliest published time, this is mandatory and doesn't need to be
shown in the body of the page, the entry format needs to comply with
ISO8601 regulations' UTC format,
like "YYYY-MM-DDTHH :MM :SS+TIMEZONE"

<meta property="article :published_time" content="2017-11-
15T08 :37 :23+07 :00" />
```

// Author Name is mandatory and needs to be shown in the page. If the content is completed by multiple authors, extra rows can be added:
<meta property="article :author" content="Nom de l'auteur #1"/>
<meta property="article :author" content="Nom de l'auteur #2" />

// Original publisher name and its URL, this optional entry is used to distinguish original and shared content.

<meta property="article :published_first" content="Nom du Blog, http://www.nom-du-blog.com/nom-article/" />

Once the code has been integrated into the pages, when Baidu recrawls the site, an "original author" mention should normally appear in the SERPs (see Figure 7.11);

Figure 7.11. *Original author in Baidu's search results (image source: Dragon Metrics)*

3) We have the possibility to automatically prioritize the indexing of URLs to Baidu as soon as they are published.

Consequently, the Chinese search engine knows who is the first author to have sent the content to its index.

To do this, you need to develop a script in JS and implement it in Baidu's Webmaster Tools to run it. Everything happens at the link submission level: 链接提交[4] (link submission).

Then, once in the section 链接提交 (link submission), select 自动提交 (automatic submission) and choose 自动推送 (automatic push).

This reminds us of the Authorship and Authorank project that Google launched between 2013 and 2014 with Google+.

It should be noted that Baidu's Spark Project has been in existence since 2013, but it was not sufficiently advanced. Now it is stable and the codes of this "Original Content Protection" project should be applied to all Chinese website content pages in order to protect them.

In Baidu's Webmaster tools, it is also possible to submit and possibly accelerate the indexing of web pages.

Baidu issued a press release[5] to share an official tip on accelerating the indexing of new pages created. Indeed, in Baidu's webmaster tools (Baidu Ziyuan), there is a tool that allows you to manually submit URLs in order to make them crawlable and indexable more quickly by the Chinese search engine.

In the article in Chinese, we can read that, following the submission of the links, the URLs should be indexed within the month. Here is the original and official communication in Chinese:

> "百度之前推出过网站登陆地址 (http://www.baidu.com/searc h/url_submit.htm) 可以提交新站点，但是提交时看到那句"符合相关标准您提交的网址，会在1个月内按百度搜索引擎收录标准被处理。
>
> 百度不保证一定能收录您提交的网站"让人有点担忧，一个月，太漫长了。"

---

4 "Submission of links", available at: http://ziyuan.baidu.com/linksubmit/ index.

5 "新站加快收录的工具——链接提交之手动提交" (Quick Indexing Tool for New Sites – Manual URL Submission), available at: https://ziyuan.baidu.com/college/articleinfo? id=1109.

Here it is translated to English:

> "Baidu has launched the interface http://www.baidu.com/
> search/url_submit.htm to submit new URLs. However during
> submission, we received a message telling us that it would take
> around one month to take the URLs into account, and Baidu
> cannot guarantee the indexation of all URLs. This may concern
> the majority of webmasters".

Thus, Baidu mentions that it is not certain to take into account (and therefore index) all URLs submitted manually.

Some webmasters find that indexing in one month is slow. If we compare with Google, the American engine has sometimes already indexed an entire site in 3 or 4 days (depending on page size, technical issues, etc.).

Here is our process for manually submitting links to index to Baidu:

1) connect to Baidu Webmaster Tools (Baidu Ziyuan), and choose 站点信息 (website information) then 链接提交 (URL submission) to find the site for which we want to submit the new pages (see Figure 7.12);

Figure 7.12. *Left menu to choose 站点信息 (website information)*

2) choose manual submission by following this path 链接提交 (URL submission) > 手动提交 (manual submission) (see Figure 7.13).

Figure 7.13. *Access menu for manual link submission*

It is only possible to submit a *maximum of 20 new URLs at a time*, as Baidu must be given time to view and index them.

In addition to Baidu's webmaster tools, there is a traffic tracking tool called Baidu Tongji. We believe it is an equivalent of Google Analytics, but it allows you to track performance and KPIs that are a little different from those of Google.

For example, Baidu Tongji also allows you to track the positions and evolution trends of ten keywords.

It should be noted that Baidu requires a processing time of approximately 24 hours before data can be uploaded to Baidu Tongji. This is another difference between Google Analytics and Baidu Tongji.

Following the keywords, is quite simple, since all you need to do is:

1) connect to Baidu Tongji;

2) go to 搜索词排名 (ranking of keywords);

3) enter the list of the top ten keywords you want to follow (see Figure 7.14);

4) wait for a processing time of 24 hours, the completion of which is announced before the data are sent back (see Figure 7.15).

设置搜索词

您最多可设置10个搜索词（词的长度不超过30个字符，由中英文和数字...

1

2

3

4

5

6

7

8

9

10

Figure 7.14. *List of keywords to follow in Baidu Tongji*

This feature is part of a fairly complete range of features found in Baidu Tongji.

There are many other Baidu tools that allow you to track website health (Baidu Webmaster Tools), track trends of interest of a keyword (Baidu Index), find popular keywords (Baidu Fengchao), etc.

Baidu is considered one of the most used and powerful search engines in the world. China is experiencing a favorable economic situation and it is therefore a market that is developing at a high speed.

SEO on Baidu and other Chinese search engines requires that we be systematically on the lookout and aware of all the latest news.

The Chinese market is evolving and changing very quickly. That is why you have to adapt and question yourself very often.

Figure 7.15. *Processing time of up to 24 hours for data feedback*

To learn more about Baidu SEO, the author of this book has written another book[6] about SEO in China only and invites anyone interested to read it.

7.2. Yandex SEO

Yandex was created in 1997 by Arkady Volozh, a computer scientist and entrepreneur. It is the most widely used engine in Russia, with a market share of 55–60% each year. Google ranks after the Russian engine.

The SEO factors for Yandex are a little different from those of Google and Baidu. The criteria that Yandex prioritize are:

– the behavior of Internet users on the site;

<hr />

6 *Baidu SEO: Challenges and Intricacies of Marketing in China*, ISTE Press, London and John Wiley & Sons, New York, 2017; available at: http://iste. co.uk/book.php?id=1172.

– the time spent on the site;

– the rebound rate;

– the quality of the content;

– the ergonomics of the site.

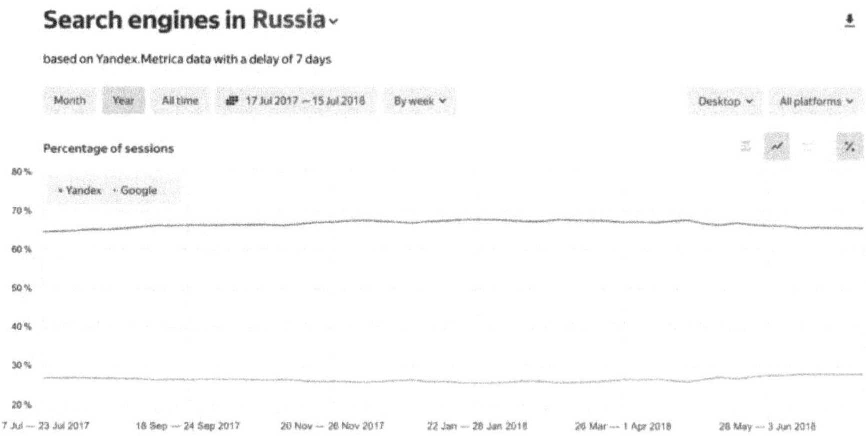
Search engines in Russia
based on Yandex.Metrica data with a delay of 7 days
Month
Year
All time
17 Jul 2017 – 15 Jul 2018
By week
Desktop
All platforms
Percentage of sessions
Yandex
Google
80 %
70 %
60 %
50 %
40 %
30 %
20 %
7 Jul – 23 Jul 2017
18 Sep – 24 Sep 2017
20 Nov – 26 Nov 2017
22 Jan – 28 Jan 2018
26 Mar – 1 Apr 2018
28 May – 3 Jun 2018

Figure 7.16. *Yandex market share (red curve) versus Google (blue curve) in 2018. For a color version of this figure, see www.iste.co.uk/duong/SEO1.zip*

They are factors related to user behaviors and signals that Yandex Metrica (the Analytics tool) could send to Yandex.

Unlike Baidu, Yandex is more similar to Google in terms of the technical parts and the consideration of some tags such as canonical tags, hreflang, meta-itemprop tags, etc.

However, in this section dedicated to Yandex, we will share the basics and new features of the Russian engine.

We will start by searching for keywords on Yandex. Indeed, Yandex (just like Google and Baidu) has its own keyword generation tool[7].

Simply enter a keyword in the field provided and click on "Submit" to get the keyword ideas and their search volumes per month (see Figure 7.17).

7 The tool is available at: https:Yandex//wordstat.yandex.com/.

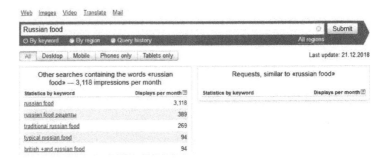

Figure 7.17. *Keyword ideas generated in Wordstat Yandex*

To better target a particular audience, we can also search or sort keywords by term, city, territory and device (computers, mobiles, tablets).

We can also look at the *search volumes* and *popularity of the keyword*, as in Google.

The study of keywords to be carried out is identical to that of Google. However, it is preferable to use the same method as Yandex to present the data, so that it corresponds to the criteria of the Russian engine (search volume per month, per type of device, etc.).

Yandex also offers tools to monitor a site's health and traffic performance. We will describe Yandex Webmaster and Yandex Metrica.

Yandex Webmaster Tools allows you to see a fairly large number of metrics, such as crawl statistics (crawl budget), external links and internal links and it sends notifications to alert you regarding technical issues on the site, such as when the robots.txt is no longer detectable, when the favicon is absent, etc. (see Figure 7.18).

Figure 7.18. *Yandex Webmaster notifications*

Figure 7.19 shows the complete menu of Yandex Webmaster Tools.

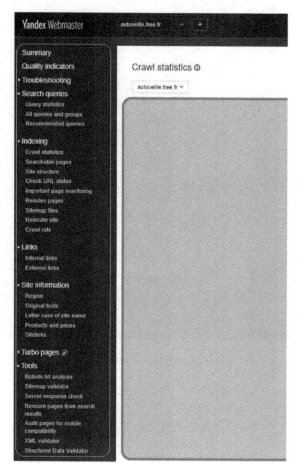

Figure 7.19. *Complete menu of Yandex Webmaster*

Yandex Webmaster Tools is a tool that is rapidly evolving and becoming more and more complete. It provides an overview of many metrics and this allows us to have accurate data on external factors, such as incoming links (the complete URL, anchor, day detected, etc.).

We also use Yandex Metrica to monitor site performance.

The site is generated with a customization at the tag name level, as shown in Figure 7.20.

```
Code snippet                                    Copy code snippet

<!-- Yandex.Metrika counter -->
<script type="text/javascript" >
    (function (d, w, c) {
        (w[c] = w[c] || []).push(function() {
            try {
                w.yaCounter51157163 = new Ya.Metrika2({
                    id:51157163,
                    clickmap:true,
                    trackLinks:true,
                    accurateTrackBounce:true
                });
            } catch(e) { }
        });

        var n = d.getElementsByTagName("script")[0],
            s = d.createElement("script"),
            f = function () { n.parentNode.insertBefore(s, n); };
        s.type = "text/javascript";
        s.async = true;
        s.src = "https://mc.yandex.ru/metrika/tag.js";

        if (w.opera == "[object Opera]") {
            d.addEventListener("DOMContentLoaded", f, false);
        } else { f(); }
    })(document, window, "yandex_metrika_callbacks2");
</script>
<noscript><div><img src="https://mc.yandex.ru/watch/51157163"
style="position:absolute; left:-9999px;" alt="" /></div></noscript>
<!-- /Yandex.Metrika counter -->
```

Figure 7.20. *Generation of the Yandex Metrica tracking code*

After pasting the code into the pages to be tracked on the site, you can track performance as in Google Analytics or Baidu Tongji.

Figure 7.21. *Setting objectives in "Settings > Goals > Conversions"*

Figure 7.22 shows the creation of the objective (possibility to enter regular expressions).

Figure 7.22. *Adding goals in Yandex Metrica*

It is possible to create up to 200 goals in Yandex Metrica, as well as the number of pages and pages to be visited by users.

On Yandex, there are different SEO criteria for indexing, crawl and finally positioning, as we mentioned earlier.

The first is related to the behavior of users on the site and the question to ask is: "Do they often come back to the site?"

The rebound rate is also an indicator. Seniority, content quality and external links also count.

We discussed the fact that Google and Baidu have each set up their own systems to create alternative mobile versions of traditional sites. Yandex also has its own process, Turbo Pages, which we will explain below.

According to our tests, Turbo Pages are faster to set up than Google's AMP or Baidu's MIP pages. The language used to create Russian mobile pages is XML and it is necessary to create an RSS feed to generate Turbo Pages.

To set up a Turbo Page, several steps are required: create the page in RSS/XML, then go to Yandex Webmaster to declare it, as well as the menu and content of the site.

Figure 7.23 shows an extract from the XML source code (RSS feed) of our Turbo Page.

```
1    <?xml version="1.0" encoding="utf-8"?>
2      <rss
3        xmlns:yandex="http://news.yandex.ru"
4        xmlns:media="http://search.yahoo.com/mrss/"
5        xmlns:turbo="http://turbo.yandex.ru"
6        version="2.0"
7      >
8      <channel>
9        <title>AUTOVEILLE | ВЕРОНИКА ДОНГ | ЭКСПЕРТ ПО ПОИСКОВОЙ ОПТИМИЗАЦИИ (SEO) В GOOGLE И BAIDU</title>
10       <link>http://autoveille.free.fr</link>
11       <description>Эксперт по поисковой оптимизации (SEO) в Google и Baidu, управляющая и главный операционн
                поисковой оптимизации (SEO), сертифицированный CESEO - Увлеченная поисковой оптимизацией с 2010 года -
                уровня,</description>
12       <turbo:analytics type="Yandex" id="51157163"></turbo:analytics>
13       <turbo:adNetwork type="AdFox" turbo-ad-id="first_ad_place">
14         <![CDATA[
15           <div id="container ID"></div>
16           <script>
17             window.Ya.adfoxCode.create({
18               ownerId: 51157163,
19               containerId: 'container ID',
20               params: {
21                 pp: 'g',
22                 ps: 'cmic',
23                 p2: 'fqem'
24               }
```

Figure 7.23. *XML source code to generate Turbo Pages*

In Yandex Webmaster, it is possible to declare the site favicon, menu and tracking codes and we can see an overview of the page rendering in Figure 7.24.

Figure 7.24. *Rendering of generated Turbo Pages*

Data sources
Accept the terms of use
Off
Turbo Pages in Search: 0
Link to source
RSS
YML β
Link to RSS
Add
Up to 1,000 item elements in each RSS crawl and up to 10 RSS feeds per website. You can create an RSS feed automatically using the plugin for your CMS. Documentation
Upload via API
Get token
Bulk upload for large sites. Up to 10,000 item elements per batch with a maximum of 10 simultaneous batches. Documentation
Type
Data source
Status
Validation date
RSS
http://autoveille.free.fr/turbo-page.rss
No errors
Off

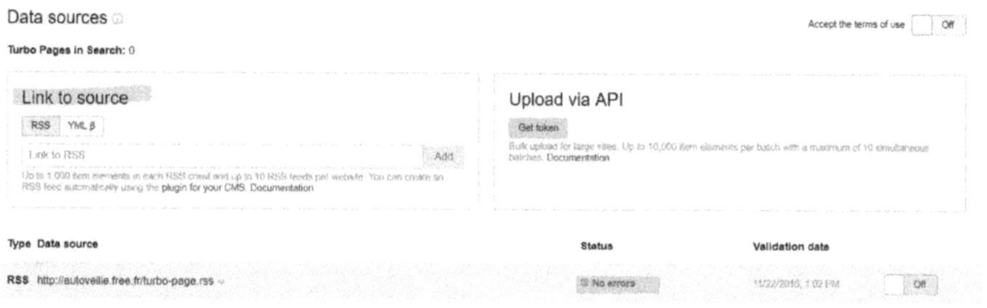

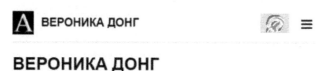

Figure 7.25. *Validation of Turbo Pages in Yandex Webmaster Data Sources*

You must then validate your Turbo Page in the data sources interface (a bit like the AMP Validator) (see Figure 7.25).

Figure 7.26 illustrates the rendering of our Turbo Page.

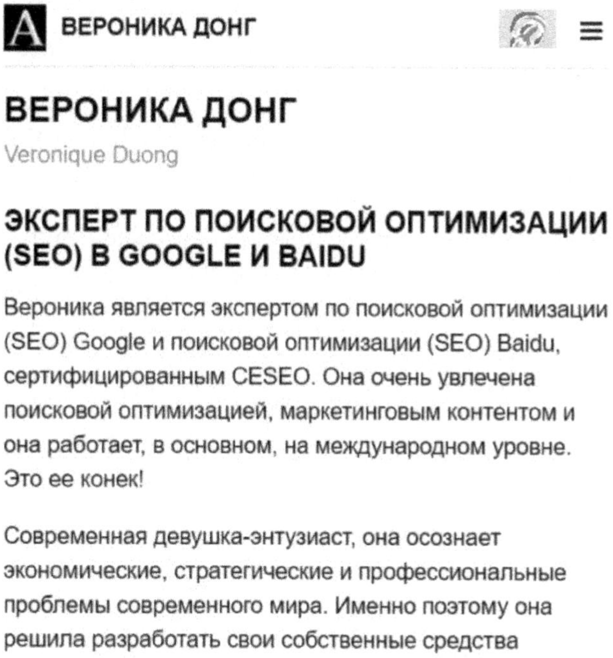

ВЕРОНИКА ДОНГ
ВЕРОНИКА ДОНГ
Veronique Duong
ЭКСПЕРТ ПО ПОИСКОВОЙ ОПТИМИЗАЦИИ (SEO) В GOOGLE И BAIDU
Вероника является экспертом по поисковой оптимизации (SEO) Google и поисковой оптимизации (SEO) Baidu, сертифицированным CESEO. Она очень увлечена поисковой оптимизацией, маркетинговым контентом и она работает, в основном, на международном уровне. Это ее конек!
Современная девушка-энтузиаст, она осознает экономические, стратегические и профессиональные проблемы современного мира. Именно поэтому она решила разработать свои собственные средства

Figure 7.26. *Rendering of the Turbo Page, refined and mobile compatible*

The Turbo Pages are marked with a symbol representing a small rocket to show that they are mobile compatible and load very quickly.

We have run our Turbo Page in a loading time tracking tool: it loads in less than 5 sec with an iPhone 6S simulation, 3G connection in Germany (see Figure 7.27).

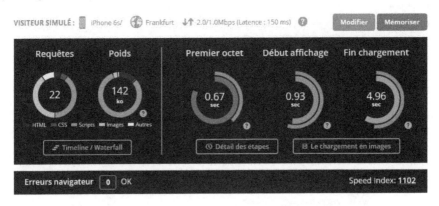

Figure 7.27. *Simulation of loading time of a Turbo Page*

The speed index is also less than 3,000 on mobile (1,102 in our case), which means that the speed signal sent to search engines is very good.

Yandex Webmaster also allows you to monitor the health of the Turbo Pages and indicates any errors encountered in the page (see Figure 7.28).

Type Data source   Status

RSS http://autoveille.free.fr/turbo-page.rss ⌃   ⊘ No errors

RSS has been validated and enabled.

When RSS is enabled, the source is re-crawled and Turbo page previews in search are updated every hour.

File last accessed
Total pages: 1
Valid: 1

Appear in search
Total pages: 1

Changelog

Preview Turbo pages in Search

Figure 7.28. *Monitoring the health of Turbo Pages*

Google, Baidu and Yandex are all dedicated to making the Web faster, by creating pages specially adapted for mobile. As we can see, they are not very esthetically pleasing, do not necessarily have many images and are very simple in terms of esthetic design.

The idea of search engines is to ensure that web pages load faster and faster and that we can access information even when connected to 3G.

7.3. Naver SEO

The South Korean search engine Naver was created in June 1999 by Naver Corporation, headed by Hae-Jin Lee, a computer engineer. We have been following the Korean search engine for years and it must be said that it has really improved in many respects. Previously, there were no tools for webmasters on Naver, no tools to track search trends, etc.

In this section, we will share our recommendations and advice to set up the basics of SEO on Naver.

In terms of market share, Naver has about 80% share each year and, according to 2018 data, Naver had an 82% market share that year (see Figure 7.29)[8].

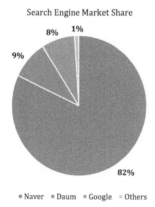

Search Engine Market Share

■ Naver   ■ Daum   ■ Google   ■ Others

Figure 7.29. *Naver's market share in South Korea (2018). For a color version of this figure, see www.iste.co.uk/duong/SEO1.zip*

8 "Naver Market Share in South Korea", available at: https://www.infocubic.co.jp/en/blog/wp-content/uploads/2018/11/Search-Engine-Market-Share-South-Korea.jpg.

As we can see, Google has only an 8% market share and each year Google has less than 10% in South Korea.

In Asia, Google is not the most suitable search engine for use. Asian Internet users have other habits, which include very rich information portals (Baidu, Qihoo 360, Yahoo! Japan, Naver, etc.).

There was a time when blogs and forums had more weight on Naver. They were systematically ranked in front of official websites, corporate sites and e-commerce. However, since the launch of Naver Webmaster Tools in the summer of 2014, the importance of blogs and forums has declined and official websites, whether corporate or e-commerce, have gained impact and weight.

Official websites now have more influence for SEO and web marketing in Korea. It is no longer be necessary to use only the blogging strategy on Naver (Cafe Naver) to generate visibility, but to focus on the SEO of classic sites[9].

As with Baidu or Yahoo! Japan (whose model is based on Google), there is no English interface for Naver's tools. Only Yandex offers an English version of these tools.

To create an account on Naver's Webmaster Tools, here is the procedure:

1) click on "sign-in" in the interface;

2) choose a user name and password;

3) the site's domain can be added to Naver Webmasters Tools and can be validated. Once the blue OK button has been clicked, a pop-up will open and it will be possible to finalize the verification of the website;

4) enter the domain name in the field, as shown in Figure 7.30;

5) check the website with one of the proposed methods, as for Google Search Console (we recommend here validating with the verification meta tags). It is necessary to add the verification meta tags in the < head> </head> part of the site;

---

9 The Naver Webmaster Tools are available at: https://webmastertool.naver.com.

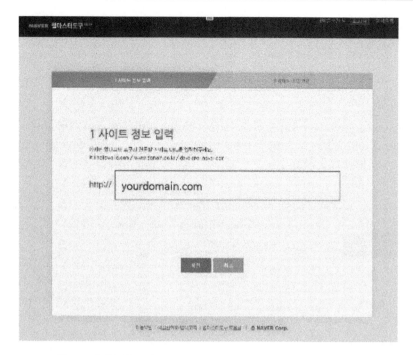

Figure 7.30. *Entering the domain name of the site in Naver*

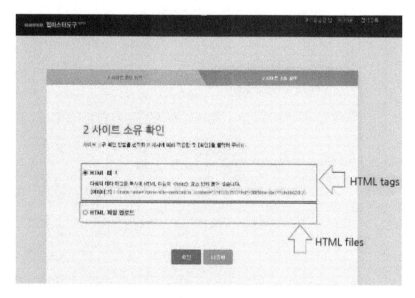

Figure 7.31. *Checking the site to be monitored in Naver Webmaster Tools*

6) return to the Naver Webmaster Tools interface;

7) click on the blue button "OK";

8) the site must return a message indicating that the domain name has been verified.

Naver allows you to track the site's crawl statistics (crawl budget), page indexing and other technical aspects related to the site's development and SEO (see Figure 7.32).

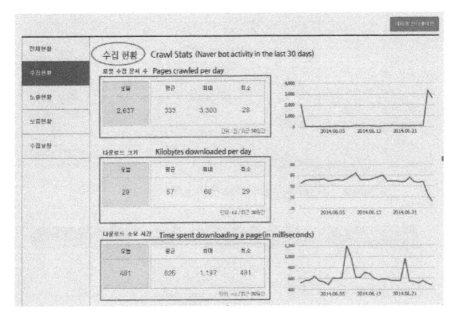

Figure 7.32. *Monitoring a site's health performance in Naver*

Naver also allows you to track the page indexing rate in your search results for a given site (see Figure 7.33).

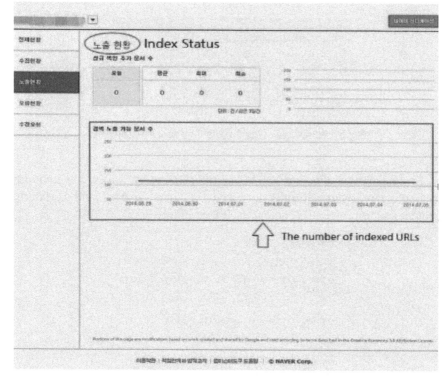

Figure 7.33. *Tracking indexed pages in Naver*

In addition, Naver also provides performance data for these different elements:

– crawl errors;

– DNS status;

– server connectivity;

– robots.txt;

– volume of crawled pages per day;

– volume of kilobytes downloaded per day;

– download time allocated for a page.

Another technical aspect is that Naver accepts Open Graph meta tags and also takes into account canonical tags.

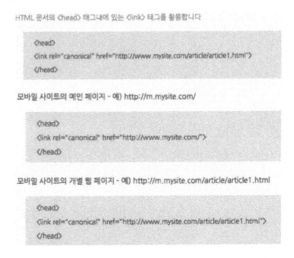

Figure 7.34. *Open Graph meta tags accepted by Naver*

Since canonical tags are also taken into account by Naver, it is important to implement them carefully to avoid duplicate internal and/or external content and to protect the content itself (see Figure 7.35).

Figure 7.35. *Canonical tags taken into account by Naver*

Like other search engines, Naver also has its own keyword generator. On the other hand, to access it, you need a paid account for sponsored ads (just like for Baidu).

Figure 7.36 provides an overview of the interface of the Naver keyword generator.

Similar to other keyword generation tools, the Naver tool also offers keyword ideas, with their search volumes, competitive potential, CPC (cost per click), etc.

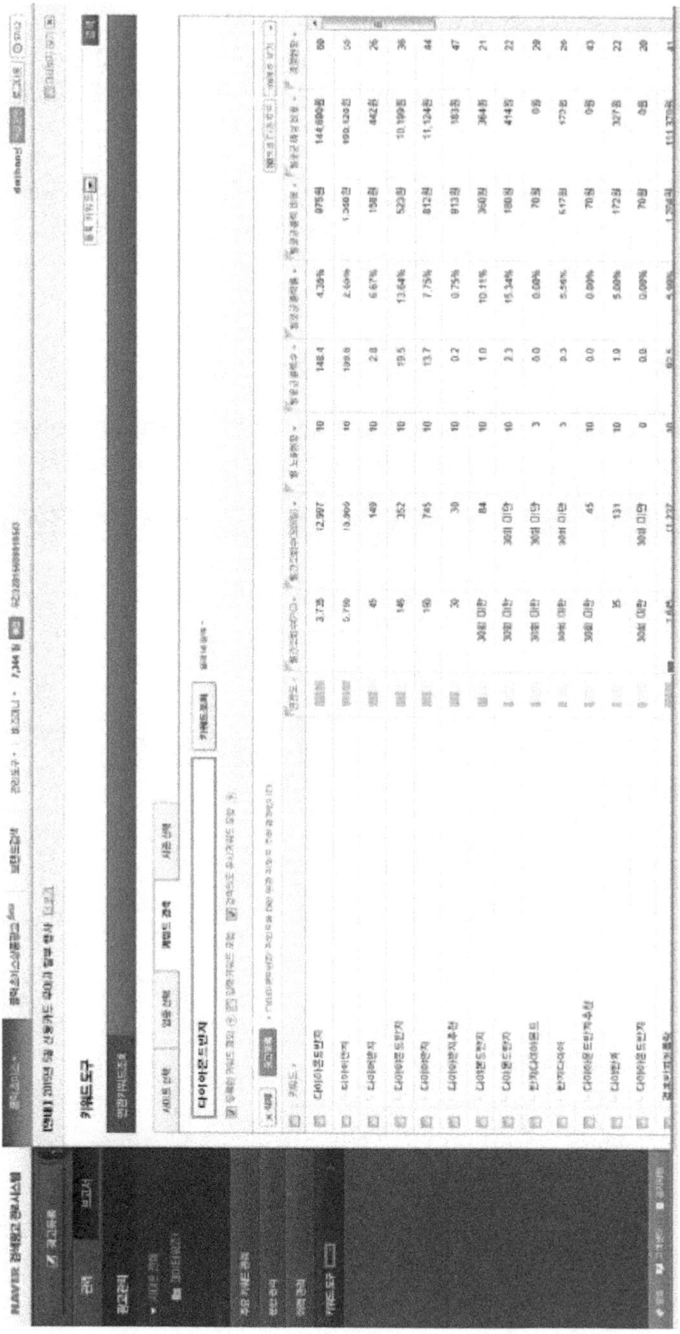

Figure 7.36. *Tool for generating Naver keywords*

Following the completion of the Korean keyword study, we can focus on the optimization of Korean meta tags. The principle is similar to Google: we still have the title and the meta description, but what counts for Naver is is the *meta keywords* tag.

There are character limits for Naver. Thus, the title and meta description officially have different lengths from Google (Asian characters have 2 or 3 bytes):

– 15 Korean characters for the title;

– 45 Korean characters for the meta description.

There is also another tool to track Naver's search interests and trends: the Naver Datalab tool, an equivalent of Google Trends (see Figure 7.37).

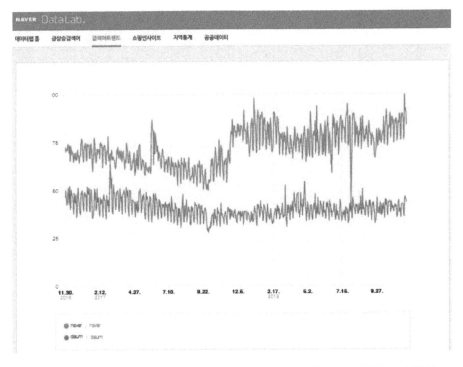

Figure 7.37. *Naver Datalab, comparing Naver to Daum between 2016 and 2018, Naver being searched on much more*

In addition, as for Baidu, it is necessary to totally localize or adapt the texts of the site to Korean and not to translate them literally.

The SEO on Naver is also very oriented toward quality content. The more we have long articles and interesting or attractive multimedia content, the more visibility, interaction and commitment we will see on our sites.

Of all the search engines we have studied throughout this book, and if we take Google as a reference, the one that least resembles Google is Baidu. Other engines like Yandex or Naver take into account some of the tags that American giants have put in place, such as canonical tags, schema.org (meta-item prop) and Open Graph.

We note that technical aspects are very important for all search engines, and each engine offers its own tools to monitor the health and performance of a site.

Today, having a site without these tools configured to track KPIs is not a good practice. We strongly recommend that they be implemented as soon as possible, if they have not yet been implemented.

Conclusion

Opening Questions

We are coming to the end of this book, where we have shared much of our experience in the field of SEO. We wanted to write a book that covers, in the most generic way possible, the whole field.

We did not want to only focus on Google, although a large part of this book is devoted to the American search engine, which is often considered as the reference.

The idea was to introduce SEO in the broadest sense and to discuss search engines that are less well-known in the West but very well-known elsewhere in the world, such as in Russia, China or South Korea.

With the progress made and linked to research and development, human–machine communication will only grow and improve from year to year.

Between mobile devices and voice speakers that already monopolize the various territories in Asia and America, those in Europe, Africa and Oceania will very soon follow this trend.

Regarding voice search via speakers or smartphones, SEO experts are pioneers who work to optimize search results, so that they correctly go back to position 0 or the featured snippet.

At the time of writing, we are still at an early stage of voice search, but we already know, through various estimates, that this is the research method of the future.

All search engines tend to become response engines. However, tests and improvements are still needed on devices such as Google Home in order to really make them assistants in everyday life, because these devices do not always understand all the questions we ask them.

The future of search and SEO will be constantly changing and we have to wonder how best to prepare ourselves in order to adapt. Will change ever be so advanced that we will no longer be able to adapt?

Natural SEO has been around for a little over 20 years and we have always managed to adapt, and we are thinking in particular of China, where everything is evolving at high speed and where facial recognition is already very advanced.

If, one day, search or SEO evolves in such a way that we have the possibility to use facial recognition to perform a search or to obtain information, we wonder if we could continue to adapt our practices.

References

Books

Andrieu, O. (2013). *Réussir son référencement web : Stratégie et techniques SEO.* Eyrolles, Paris.

Canivet, I. (2011). *Bien rédiger pour le web : Stratégie de contenu pour améliorer son référencement naturel.* Eyrolles, Paris.

Chartier, M. (2013). *Le Guide du référencement web.* First Interactive, Paris.

Duong, V. (2017). *Baidu SEO: Challenges and Intricacies of Marketing in China.* ISTE Ltd., London and John Wiley & Sons, New York.

Martin, A., Chartier, M. (2014). *Techniques de référencement web : Audit et suivi SEO.* Eyrolles, Paris.

Websites

Abondance: https://www.abondance.com.

Autoveille: https://autoveille.info.

Baidu Tongji: https://tongji.baidu.com.

Baidu Ziyuan: https://ziyuan.baidu.com.

Dragon Metrics: https://www.dragonmetrics.com/blog.

Google Adwords: https://ads.google.com.

Google Trends: https://trends.google.fr.

Naver Datalab: https://datalab.naver.com/keyword/trendSearch.naver.

Naver Webmaster Tools: https://webmastertool.naver.com.

Pending.schema.org: https://pending.schema.org/speakable.

Schema.org: https://schema.org.

SEO Camp: https://www.seo-camp.org.

Support Google: https://support.google.com.

WebRankInfo: https://www.webrankinfo.com.

Yandex Metrica: https://metrica.yandex.com.

Yandex Webmaster: https://webmaster.yandex.com.

Index

Other titles from

in

Information Systems, Web and Pervasive Computing

2019

ALBAN Daniel, EYNAUD Philippe, MALAURENT Julien, RICHET Jean-Loup, VITARI Claudio
Information Systems Management: Governance, Urbanization and Alignment

AUGEY Dominique, with the collaboration of ALCARAZ Marina
Digital Information Ecosystems: Smart Press

BATTON-HUBERT Mireille, DESJARDIN Eric, PINET François
Geographic Data Imperfection 1: From Theory to Applications

BRIQUET-DUHAZÉ Sophie, TURCOTTE Catherine
From Reading-Writing Research to Practice

BROCHARD Luigi, KAMATH Vinod, CORBALAN Julita, HOLLAND Scott, MITTELBACH Walter, OTT Michael
Energy-Efficient Computing and Data Centers

CHAMOUX Jean-Pierre
The Digital Era 2: Political Economy Revisited

COCHARD Gérard-Michel
Introduction to Stochastic Processes and Simulation

GAUCHEREL Cédric, GOUYON Pierre-Henri, DESSALLES Jean-Louis
Information, The Hidden Side of Life

GHLALA Riadh
Analytic SQL in SQL Server 2014/2016

JANIER Mathilde, SAINT-DIZIER Patrick
Argument Mining: Linguistic Foundations

SOURIS Marc
Epidemiology and Geography: Principles, Methods and Tools of Spatial Analysis

TOUNSI Wiem
Cyber-Vigilance and Digital Trust: Cyber Security in the Era of Cloud Computing and IoT

2018

ARDUIN Pierre-Emmanuel
Insider Threats
(Advances in Information Systems Set – Volume 10)

CARMÈS Maryse
Digital Organizations Manufacturing: Scripts, Performativity and Semiopolitics
(Intellectual Technologies Set – Volume 5)

CARRÉ Dominique, VIDAL Geneviève
Hyperconnectivity: Economical, Social and Environmental Challenges
(Computing and Connected Society Set – Volume 3)

CHAMOUX Jean-Pierre
The Digital Era 1: Big Data Stakes

DOUAY Nicolas
Urban Planning in the Digital Age
(Intellectual Technologies Set – Volume 6)

SZONIECKY Samuel
Ecosystems Knowledge: Modeling and Analysis Method for Information and Communication
(Digital Tools and Uses Set – Volume 6)

2017

BOUHAÏ Nasreddine, SALEH Imad
Internet of Things: Evolutions and Innovations
(Digital Tools and Uses Set – Volume 4)

DUONG Véronique
Baidu SEO: Challenges and Intricacies of Marketing in China

LESAS Anne-Marie, MIRANDA Serge
The Art and Science of NFC Programming
(Intellectual Technologies Set – Volume 3)

LIEM André
Prospective Ergonomics
(Human-Machine Interaction Set – Volume 4)

MARSAULT Xavier
Eco-generative Design for Early Stages of Architecture
(Architecture and Computer Science Set – Volume 1)

REYES-GARCIA Everardo
The Image-Interface: Graphical Supports for Visual Information
(Digital Tools and Uses Set – Volume 3)

REYES-GARCIA Everardo, BOUHAÏ Nasreddine
Designing Interactive Hypermedia Systems
(Digital Tools and Uses Set – Volume 2)

SAÏD Karim, BAHRI KORBI Fadia
Asymmetric Alliances and Information Systems:Issues and Prospects
(Advances in Information Systems Set – Volume 7)

SZONIECKY Samuel, BOUHAÏ Nasreddine
Collective Intelligence and Digital Archives: Towards Knowledge Ecosystems
(Digital Tools and Uses Set – Volume 1)

2016

BEN CHOUIKHA Mona
Organizational Design for Knowledge Management

BERTOLO David
Interactions on Digital Tablets in the Context of 3D Geometry Learning
(Human-Machine Interaction Set – Volume 2)

BOUVARD Patricia, SUZANNE Hervé
Collective Intelligence Development in Business

EL FALLAH SEGHROUCHNI Amal, ISHIKAWA Fuyuki, HÉRAULT Laurent, TOKUDA Hideyuki
Enablers for Smart Cities

FABRE Renaud, in collaboration with MESSERSCHMIDT-MARIET Quentin, HOLVOET Margot
New Challenges for Knowledge

GAUDIELLO Ilaria, ZIBETTI Elisabetta
Learning Robotics, with Robotics, by Robotics
(Human-Machine Interaction Set – Volume 3)

HENROTIN Joseph
The Art of War in the Network Age
(Intellectual Technologies Set – Volume 1)

KITAJIMA Munéo
Memory and Action Selection in Human–Machine Interaction
(Human–Machine Interaction Set – Volume 1)

LAGRAÑA Fernando
E-mail and Behavioral Changes: Uses and Misuses of Electronic Communications

LEIGNEL Jean-Louis, UNGARO Thierry, STAAR Adrien
Digital Transformation
(Advances in Information Systems Set – Volume 6)

NOYER Jean-Max
Transformation of Collective Intelligences
(Intellectual Technologies Set – Volume 2)

VENTRE Daniel
Information Warfare – 2ⁿᵈ edition

VITALIS André
The Uncertain Digital Revolution
(Computing and Connected Society Set – Volume 1)

2015

ARDUIN Pierre-Emmanuel, GRUNDSTEIN Michel, ROSENTHAL-SABROUX Camille
Information and Knowledge System
(Advances in Information Systems Set – Volume 2)

BÉRANGER Jérôme
Medical Information Systems Ethics

BRONNER Gérald
Belief and Misbelief Asymmetry on the Internet

IAFRATE Fernando
From Big Data to Smart Data
(Advances in Information Systems Set – Volume 1)

KRICHEN Saoussen, BEN JOUIDA Sihem
Supply Chain Management and its Applications in Computer Science

NEGRE Elsa
Information and Recommender Systems
(Advances in Information Systems Set – Volume 4)

POMEROL Jean-Charles, EPELBOIN Yves, THOURY Claire
MOOCs

SALLES Maryse
Decision-Making and the Information System
(Advances in Information Systems Set – Volume 3)

SAMARA Tarek
ERP and Information Systems: Integration or Disintegration
(Advances in Information Systems Set – Volume 5)

2014

DINET Jérôme
Information Retrieval in Digital Environments

HÉNO Raphaële, CHANDELIER Laure
3D Modeling of Buildings: Outstanding Sites

KEMBELLEC Gérald, CHARTRON Ghislaine, SALEH Imad
Recommender Systems

MATHIAN Hélène, SANDERS Lena
Spatio-temporal Approaches: Geographic Objects and Change Process

PLANTIN Jean-Christophe
Participatory Mapping

VENTRE Daniel
Chinese Cybersecurity and Defense

2013

BERNIK Igor
Cybercrime and Cyberwarfare

CAPET Philippe, DELAVALLADE Thomas
Information Evaluation

LEBRATY Jean-Fabrice, LOBRE-LEBRATY Katia
Crowdsourcing: One Step Beyond

SALLABERRY Christian
Geographical Information Retrieval in Textual Corpora

2012

BUCHER Bénédicte, LE BER Florence
Innovative Software Development in GIS

GAUSSIER Eric, YVON François
Textual Information Access

STOCKINGER Peter
Audiovisual Archives: Digital Text and Discourse Analysis

VENTRE Daniel
Cyber Conflict

2011

BANOS Arnaud, THÉVENIN Thomas
Geographical Information and Urban Transport Systems

DAUPHINÉ André
Fractal Geography

LEMBERGER Pirmin, MOREL Mederic
Managing Complexity of Information Systems

STOCKINGER Peter
Introduction to Audiovisual Archives

STOCKINGER Peter
Digital Audiovisual Archives

VENTRE Daniel
Cyberwar and Information Warfare

2010

BONNET Pierre
Enterprise Data Governance

BRUNET Roger
Sustainable Geography

CARREGA Pierre
Geographical Information and Climatology

CAUVIN Colette, ESCOBAR Francisco, SERRADJ Aziz
Thematic Cartography – 3-volume series
Thematic Cartography and Transformations – Volume 1
Cartography and the Impact of the Quantitative Revolution – Volume 2
New Approaches in Thematic Cartography – Volume 3

LANGLOIS Patrice
Simulation of Complex Systems in GIS

MATHIS Philippe
Graphs and Networks – 2ⁿᵈ edition

THERIAULT Marius, DES ROSIERS François
Modeling Urban Dynamics

2009

BONNET Pierre, DETAVERNIER Jean-Michel, VAUQUIER Dominique
Sustainable IT Architecture: the Progressive Way of Overhauling
Information Systems with SOA

PAPY Fabrice
Information Science

RIVARD François, ABOU HARB Georges, MERET Philippe
The Transverse Information System

ROCHE Stéphane, CARON Claude
Organizational Facets of GIS

2008

BRUGNOT Gérard
Spatial Management of Risks

FINKE Gerd
Operations Research and Networks

GUERMOND Yves
Modeling Process in Geography

KANEVSKI Michael
Advanced Mapping of Environmental Data

MANOUVRIER Bernard, LAURENT Ménard
Application Integration: EAI, B2B, BPM and SOA

PAPY Fabrice
Digital Libraries

2007

DOBESCH Hartwig, DUMOLARD Pierre, DYRAS Izabela
Spatial Interpolation for Climate Data

SANDERS Lena
Models in Spatial Analysis

2006

CLIQUET Gérard
Geomarketing

CORNIOU Jean-Pierre
Looking Back and Going Forward in IT

DEVILLERS Rodolphe, JEANSOULIN Robert
Fundamentals of Spatial Data Quality